CRYING

FOR A DREAM

CRYING
FOR A DREAM

*The World Through
Native American Eyes*

by

RICHARD ERDOES

BEAR & COMPANY
PUBLISHING
SANTA FE, NEW MEXICO

To my son, Erich,
who shared the magic hours.

LIBRARY OF CONGRESS CATALOGING-IN-PUBLICATION DATA

Erdoes, Richard.
    Crying for a dream: the world through native american eyes
        p.   cm.
    ISBN 0-939680-57-2
        1. Teton Indians—Pictorial works. 2. Indians of North America-
Great Plains—Pictorial works. I. Title
E99. T34E73 1989
987'.004975—dc20   89-33924
                                                            CIP

Bear & Company
Santa Fe, NM 87504-2860

Cover and interior design: Kathleen Katz
Photography: Richard Erdoes
Editing: Gail Vivino
Photo Editing: Barbara Hand Clow and Angela C. Werneke
Typography: Casa Sin Nombre
Printed in the United States of America by Arcata Graphics

9 8 7 6 5 4 3 2 1

TABLE OF CONTENTS

Acknowledgments   vi

Preface   1

PART ONE: CRYING FOR A DREAM   7

     Dancing For A Better World   8

     The Indians' Flesh And Blood   17

     Fire Without End   19

     Going Upon The Hill   24

     Little Lights In The Dark   30

     He Has No Eyes But He Sees   36

     A Sound Of Eaglebone Whistles   41

PART TWO: DEFENDING THE DREAM   49

     I Want The White Man Beside Me,
     Not Above Me   50

PART THREE: LIVING THE DREAM   63

     People Of The Plains   70

     People Of The Mesas   86

     People Of The Desert   106

About the Author   120

Bibliography   121

ACKNOWLEDGMENTS

I thank all those native friends, both the living and those who have gone to the spirit world, for giving me a glimpse of their wisdom and their thoughts.

PREFACE

All Sioux ceremonies end with the words, *mitakuye oyasin*—"all my relations"—meaning every living human being on this Earth, every plant and animal, down to the smallest flower and tiniest bug.

The Indians' relationship to the Earth, the winds, and the animals is intimate and intensely personal, closely related to their sacred beliefs. This relationship arises out of their environment, the hills and trees around them, the prairie or desert upon which they walk. It arises out of their nature-related language and out of age-old oral traditions passed on from generation to generation.

Some fifteen years ago, together with my friend, the Sioux medicine man, Lame Deer, I took part in a panel discussion on Indian religion. A missionary priest turned to Lame Deer and said, "Chief, I respect your beliefs. My church is built in the shape of a tipi, my vestments are beaded, the Sacred Pipe hangs next to the cross on my wall. I participate in Indian ceremonies. I tell you—The Great Spirit and God are the same. Sweet Medicine and Christ are the same. The Pipe and the cross, they are all the same. There is no real difference between your and my religions."

Lame Deer looked at the missionary for some time and then said, "Father, in your religion do animals have a soul?"

The priest answered with a slightly embarrassed smile, "Chief, you got me there!"

On another occasion my friend was interviewed by a rather belligerent lady who taunted him, saying, "Lame Deer, you say that you speak to animals. Come on! This is the twentieth century. Don't put me on!"

Lame Deer grinned: "Lady, in your Good Book a woman talks to a snake but *I speak with eagles!*"

Another Native American told me, "Us Indians and the Blacks have the same problem living under the White Man, but there is one big difference: they want *in*, we want *out!*"

The native's view of the universe is very unlike that of his or her white fellow-Americans. There is White Man's time and Indian time—Moon time or orbit time. An Indian acquires fame by giving possessions away, while whites acquire more and more property as their status symbols. Whites, if at all religious, devote an hour or two to their church on a Sunday. Native Americans live their religion twenty-four hours a day, "walking in a sacred manner." When eating, Lakota people always put a morsel aside for the spirits of their departed friends. "Even while making love to a woman," Lame Deer once said, "you are doing something sacred." He, as well as many other traditionals, maintains that the Indian's symbol is the circle, the White Man's the square.

"We are bound in the Sacred Hoop—humans, the four-legged, the living green things," said Crow Dog, a Lakota spiritual man. "Orbits within orbits, circles within circles, from the Great Hoop of the universe which, eons ago, dreamed itself into existence, to the blood circles within your own body. The universe and the Earth are round. Round is the camp circle, round the tipi with the humans forming a circle within it. Round is the human hoop of the ghost dancers holding hands—circling, circling, circling until they fall down in a swoon."

"The *wasichu* [White Man] is all square," Lame Deer added. "Square is his house and its rooms. Square is the Green Frogskin, his dollar bill. Square is his mind. It has sharp corners."

"We think that certain things are alive which the White Man looks upon as dead," Jenny Leading Cloud, a Rosebud Sioux, once explained. "We think of certain rocks and trees as having a life and a soul. The Morning Star once made love to a human maiden."

"The Sacred Pipe," says Wallace Black Elk, "while we are smoking it, is alive—the flesh, blood and mind of the Indian."

Hand in hand with such concepts goes the native idea of "power." "When I held the Buffalo Calf Pipe," said Crow Dog, "I felt it moving in my hands, felt its Power flowing from it into my veins."

There is power in a pebble, in gopher dust, in an eagle wing, in the smoke rising from the pipe bowl, in a braid of sweet grass. "I just cedared you up and fanned you with my eagle wing," Lame Deer once told me, "and that way gave you a little of my power to help you doing our book."

A grandfather might give his power to a grandson, showing spiritual understanding. A medicine person might take away power from somebody who is misusing it. In the words of Lame Deer: "There is power in a wild buffalo. There is no power in a White-Man-bred Angus or Holstein."

The special relationship of the Indian to nature shows itself in the native language. The Great Spirit is referred to as Tunkashila—Grandfather. The sky is Father, the Earth Unchi—Grandmother—whose hair should not be cut by axe or sickle, nor her body injured by spade or plow. The buffalo is the people's brother. White Buffalo Woman, the Lakota culture heroine who brought the Sacred Pipe to the tribes and taught them the right way to live, appears first as a beautiful woman in shining buckskin who, when taking leave of the people, transforms herself into a white buffalo calf. The sacred herb used sacramentally by those belonging to the Native American Church is referred to as "Grandfather Peyote." The Sacred Sundance Pole is addressed as if it were a warrior. It is "captured." Its captors are counting coup upon it. It is prayed and sung to by the people. The name a person receives at his or her first vision quest is usually that of an animal, plant, or phenomenon of nature. . .White Hawk, Cedar, or Yellow Thunder.

Humanity's relationship to a living universe extends beyond the Earth. Very old people, who during their childhood were told stories by the ghost dancers of 1890, passed them on to their children and grandchildren. Many of these narratives tell of a dancer falling down in a trance, dying, and then coming to life again. Upon awakening, men and women spoke of having traveled to the Moon or to the Morning Star, coming back with "Star Flesh" in their clenched fists, flesh of the planets which had been turned into strange rocks. In some traditional families, these souvenirs from another world had been carefully preserved and, at the time of the American moonwalk, were brought out, some from within medicine bundles, the owners convinced that these were Moon rocks. As Old Fool Bull said: "We have been on the Moon long before the wasichu and we didn't need any rockets to get there."

"Don't hurt the trees, the seas, or the Earth," pray the people during a peyote meeting. Native Americans are intensely aware of a deteriorating environment, of polluted streams, evil rains, and poisoned air. A Hopi prophecy, as Thomas Benyacya, spokesman for the Hopi Nation, once related, predicts a possible end of an abused and plundered world "when a black sun rises in the East and the Hopis go to the House of Mica." Traveling to the United Nations in New York to warn of a coming Earth catastrophe, the Hopis passed Gary, Indiana, and saw a sun rising, blackened by the soot and smog from the industrialized city. Arriving in New York, they recognized in the United Nations Building the "House of Mica" mentioned in their prophecies. Similar foretellings of our world being replaced by another, worthier one, unless the people inhabiting it change their heedless ways, occur in many tribes from Meso-America all the way north to the Arctic. Some traditional men and women are saying, "White Man, better watch your step!"

This book intends to show the world as seen through Indian eyes—the sacred and the profane, the good and the bad, the extraordinary and the humdrum, things alive and things dead which, upon closer look, might not be all that dead. It stresses the differences in life philosophy between two worlds living intermingled upon this Turtle Continent. The text consists of the words of those depicted in the photographs, taken from tapes collected over a period of some twenty years.

Most of the images are those of close friends. Some of the old spiritual Plains people actually asked me to make a complete sequence of shots of certain, rarely performed ceremonies, so that after they were gone, there would still be a record of how the rituals were properly performed. I always respected the rules of those tribes which forbade the taking of photographs of sacred dances and other rites, and was always somewhat in awe and had a feeling of trespassing when asked to record Plains tribes' ceremonies.

The photographs and captions are grouped together in relation to subject matter, but the whole is held together by the concept of the all-compassing Sacred Hoop. In the words of a Lakota holy man:

There is a word meaning "All My Relations."
We will live by this word.
We are related to everything.
We are still here!
We shall live!
Mitakuye Oyasin

Henry eagle-dancing.

I used to eagle-dance. I could dance so good, people forgot I'm a human being and think I'm *wanbli*, the eagle. That's the way I moved, slowly, cocking my head. When I danced that way I felt sacred. I feel I'm an eagle and, while I dance I am an eagle. I had those huge eagle wings. I sang the soaring song. I don't do that anymore. Why? I was broke and had to sell my eagle wings.

Henry Crow Dog, 1981

Bird of prey against sunset.

CRYING FOR
A DREAM

(ceremony)

That TV interviewer, that woman with the orange-dyed hair, told me: "Lame Deer, don't put us on—being able to talk to animals. Come on. This is the 20th century!" I told her: "Lady, in your Good Book a woman talks to a snake. I, at least, talk to hawks, and falcons, and eagles."

Lame Deer, in Cleveland, 1972

7

DANCING FOR
A BETTER WORLD

The Ghost Dance, *Wanagi Wachipi*, did not originate among the Sioux but was "given" to them in 1889 by Wovoka, a Paiute prophet and dreamer from Pyramid Lake, Nevada. It was not a typical Native American dance. Men and women performed it by moving in a circle, holding hands, which is the White Man's way, not the Indian way. Its doctrine combined Christian and Indian beliefs. The Ghost Dance was a dance of desperation, born of hunger and oppression. This is expressed by one Arapaho Ghost Dance song:

> My Father, have pity on me!
> I have nothing to eat,
> I am dying of thirst—
> Everything is gone!

But the Ghost Dance was also born of hope. By performing it according to Wovoka's instruction, the dancers hoped to bring their dead relatives back to life, to bring back the buffalo nearly exterminated by white hide hunters, and to roll up the world spoiled by the White Man, together with its barbed wire fences, factories, and telegraph poles, to reveal beneath it once again the beautiful unspoiled world of the Indian, teeming with game of every kind. The anthropologist James Mooney, who had been able to interview Wovoka and many of the Ghost Dance leaders, sympathized:

"As it is with men, so it is with nations. The Lost Paradise is the world's dreamland of youth. What tribe or people has not had its golden age, before Pandora's Box was loosed, when women were nymphs and dryads, and men were gods and heros? And when a race lies crushed and groaning beneath an alien joke, how natural is the dream of a redeemer who shall return from exile or awaken from some long sleep to drive out the usurper and win back for his people what they have lost . . ."

Wovoka, the "Cutter," had worked as a hired hand for a white rancher named Wilson, listened to his reading from the bible, learned about Jesus, and watched the white folks at their round dances. During an eclipse of the sun, which sowed terror throughout the tribes, Wovoka fell seriously ill, became delirious, and lost consciousness. After he regained consciousness, he told his people:

"When the Sun died, I went to heaven and saw God and all the people who had died a long time ago. God told me to come back and tell the people they must be good and love one another, and not fight, or steal, or lie. He gave me this dance to give to my people."

The news of the new messianic religion spread like wildfire from tribe to tribe. Soon the Kiowas, Comanches, Cheyennes, Arapahos, and Shoshonis were ghost-dancing. The Sioux were electrified when word of Wovoka's prophecy reached them. The people's spirits were then at their lowest point. Fenced in on their reservations, many were dying of starvation. They had been forced onto arid land where nothing would grow. Their government rations were stolen by greedy officials and traders. They were forced to eat the seed corn that had been given to them by the agents, and to butcher the few cattle they had received, including the stud bulls. In their weakened condition, they fell victim to grippe, influenza, measles, and whooping cough, "dying like flies." Even General Miles had to admit:

"They [the Sioux] signed away a valuable portion of their reservation, and it is now occupied by white people, for which they have received nothing. They understood that ample provision would be made for their support; instead their supplies have been reduced and much of the time they have been living on half rations. Their crops, as well as the crops of white people, for two years have been almost a total failure. The disaffection is widespread, especially among the Sioux, while the Cheyennes have been on the verge of starvation and were forced to commit depredations to sustain life. These facts are beyond question and sustained by thousands of witnesses."

The Lakota were clutching at straws. When whisperings reached them of a new dance which would "make everything right again," they decided to find out about it and sent two men to speak with the Paiute holy man. These messengers were Short Bull, an aristocratic-looking Brulé from Rosebud, and Kicking Bear, a scowling warrior from the Cheyenne River Reservation. It was a great feat for them to travel hundreds of miles over fences and railroad tracks, through farmlands and around cities occupied by whites, without being detected. When they finally met Wovoka, he showed them his hat and in it they saw the whole world, their dead relatives alive and smiling, the prairie covered with buffalo. Wovoka also gave them sacred red facepaint and magpie feathers, telling them to use these in their dance. When the two messengers came back, they told the people:

"What you heard is true. Wovoka is truly *wakan—lila wakan*. His dance is good."

And so the Sioux began to ghost-dance. They made themselves special shirts covered with the images of Sun, Moon, stars, crosses, magpies, and eagles, hoping that these would make them bulletproof. They also wrapped themselves in American flags, worn upside down as a sign of distress.

Though the dance was peaceful, hysteria and fear swept the white communities around the reservations. The new religion, it was rumored, was an incitement to murder all wasichus within the territory. Royer, the agent at Pine Ridge, lost his head and wired General Miles:

"Indians are dancing in the snow and are wild and crazy. I have fully informed you that the employees and government proper at this agency have no protection and we need it now.... Nothing short of 1,000 soldiers will settle this dancing." He got three thousand.

It had not helped that an agent on an adjacent reservation had remarked: "When the holy rollers ascend trees and rooftops to await the Second Coming, nobody calls for the military." His was a voice crying in the wilderness.

Kicking Bear went to Standing Rock, the reservation of the Hunkpapa Sioux, and there persuaded Sitting Bull to let him inaugurate the Ghost Dance under the great chief's protection. Sitting Bull had long been a thorn in the side of the reservation agent, James McLaughlin, who looked upon him as "a stubborn, recalcitrant, unreconstructed, and irreconcilable heathen, standing in the way of civilization and Christianity." In the Ghost Dance, McLaughlin saw his chance to get rid of the man who still resisted the "whitemanizing" of his people. The agent sent a telegram to Washington:

"Everything quiet at present; weather cold and snowing. Am I authorized to arrest Sitting Bull and other fomentors of mischief when I think best?"

In the meantime, the dancing went on. In expectation of the buffalo's return, the people were singing:

> Somebody brought the news:
> There will be a buffalo hunt.
> There will be a buffalo hunt.
> Make arrows, make arrows!
>
> Somebody brought the news:
> They are already butchering over there.
> They are already butchering over there.
> Make arrows, make arrows!

While in trance, some of the dancers met Jesus and saw that he was an Indian. Thus a man called Tashunke Chikala, Little Horse, related: "Two holy eagles transported me to the Happy Hunting Grounds. They showed me the Great Messiah there, and as I looked upon his fair countenance I wept, for there were nail-prints in his hands and feet where the cruel whites had once fastened him to a large cross.... He insisted that we continue dancing, and promised me that no whites should enter his city nor partake of the good things he had prepared for the Indians. The earth, he said, was now worn out and it should be repeopled."

McLaughlin sent Sitting Bull a message forbidding any further ghost-dancing. The chief responded by saying that, as he did not tell the whites how to worship, they, likewise, had no right to interfere with Indian religion. McLaughlin now had the desired excuse for Sitting Bull's arrest. He ordered Lieutenant Bull Head, chief of the Indian police, to go and bring in the trouble-maker. The agent must have known that this amounted to a death sentence, because there had always been bad blood between the "metal breasts," as the tribal police were called, and Sitting Bull's followers.

Bull Head assembled 26 policemen and 2 sergeants—Shave Head and Red Tomahawk. Together with volunteers, his force numbered 43 armed men. Before sunrise, on December 15, 1890, they surrounded Sitting Bull's one-room log cabin. They went inside and told Sitting Bull that he was under arrest. "All right, all right," said the chief, who had slept naked under his buffalo robe, "I'm coming, just let me put on my clothes." The police hustled him along, pulling and pushing him. A woman's voice was heard singing:

> Tatanka Iyotake,
> Sitting Bull,
> You were a warrior once.
> What are you going to do now?

Sitting Bull began to struggle, saying, "I won't go!" The police had their guns out. Sitting Bull's closest friend, Catch the Bear, drew a Winchester from under his blanket and fired into Bull Head's side. Fatally wounded, the lieutenant sent a bullet into Sitting Bull's side while Red Tomahawk shot him in the head. General firing broke out. Sitting Bull's horse, a gift from Buffalo Bill, thought it was back in the Wild West Show and began to dance and do tricks. The desperate fight lasted only a few short minutes, but when it was over six policemen lay dead or dying, among them Bull Head and Shave Head. Of their opponents, eight had been killed, including Sitting Bull and Catch the Bear. To avenge their losses, some of the police went into the cabin and murdered the chief's seventeen-year-old son Crow Foot, despite the fact that he begged them to spare him. McLaughlin had achieved his purpose: the great holy man of the Lakotas was dead.

Regular troops arrived and fired shells into Sitting Bull's camp. His followers fled. Many of them arrived downhearted, cold, and hungry at the camp of Siha-Tanka, Big Foot, chief of the Minneconjou Sioux at Cheyenne River, spreading fear far and wide. Big Foot, described as "wise and mild-mannered, a peacemaker," was afraid that he and his people would also be attacked. He decided to take his Minneconjous, together with the Hunkpapa refugees, to Pine Ridge, seeking shelter with Red Cloud and his Oglalas. He also put himself under the protection of the military, but he had the misfortune to be stopped by troopers of the Seventh Cavalry, Custer's old outfit, which still contained many officers and men who had survived the Little Bighorn disaster. These troopers thought they had found an opportunity to settle an old score. That Big Foot's band was without arms except for a few outmoded guns, and that it consisted for the greater part of old folks, women, and children, did not bother them. As the soldiers were to sing later:

> The Red Skins left their agency, the soldiers left their post,
> All on the strength of an Indian tale about Messiah's ghost.
> Got up by savage chieftains to lead their tribes astray;
> But Uncle Sam wouldn't have it so, 'cause he ain't built that way.
> They swore that this Messiah came in a vision's sleep,
> And promised to restore their game and buffalo a heap,
> They claimed the shirt Messiah gave, no bullet could get through,
> But when the soldiers fired they found it wasn't true.
> We fired our cannon, unwarned by trumpet call,
> The Sioux were dropping man by man, the Seventh killed them all.

Big Foot was traveling in a wagon, near death from pneumonia. Through an interpreter, the sick man explained to the officer in charge that he and his Minneconjous were headed for Pine Ridge to give themselves up. He was told to go to Wounded Knee and camp there. Big Foot said he would do as told. They shook hands. When the Minneconjou reached their campsite, they were promptly surrounded by formations of the Seventh Cavalry, supported by a battery of quick-firing Hotchkiss guns which were posted on a height overlooking the Indians' camp. In the evening, the officers had a high old time getting into a keg of whiskey "to keep warm."

At daybreak, on December 29th, everything seemed to go well. Some Indians and soldiers commingled, trying to communicate. The Minneconjou wanted only to keep out of trouble and get to Pine Ridge. They were told their men must first give up their guns. A few old firearms were produced. The whites thought that there must be more. Colonel Forsyth, commanding the Seventh, ordered the tents and persons of the Indians searched. Some soldiers tried to search the women underneath their blankets. A cranky old man, called Yellow Bird, began to cackle angrily while throwing dust at the soldiers. Some young men resisted being searched. A shot was fired, nobody knew by whom. Instantly the soldiers began to empty their carbines into the mass of Indians. In the words of one officer:

"I never in my life saw Springfields worked so industriously as on this occasion."

Then the Hotchkiss guns opened up, killing scores of Indian

women and children standing in front of their tents. An officer walked up to the helpless Big Foot and shot him dead. The Indians tried to find shelter in a ravine—warriors, old people, women, children, ponies, and dogs all mixed together. The soldiers pursued them in a frenzy of killing. In the words of Mooney:

"The Hotchkiss guns poured in two-pound explosive shells at the rate of nearly 50 a minute, mowing down everything alive.... There can be no question that the pursuit was simply a massacre, where fleeing women, with their infants in their arms, were shot down after all resistance had ceased."

The flute-maker Dick Fool Bull, when he was about one hundred years old, told me that as a young boy he had been camping with his parents halfway between Wounded Knee and Pine Ridge. He heard the firing and later saw some things he had been trying to forget ever since, such as a baby nursing at the breast of its dead mother. Twenty-nine soldiers died, including one officer who had ridden with Custer, some hit in the crossfire of their own comrades. Of the Indians, some three hundred were killed. Frozen stiff and stacked like cordwood, they were buried in a common ditch.

Black Elk, who had seen the "butchered women and children lying heaped in the crooked gulch," lamented that Wounded Knee had killed a people's dreams, had broken the Lakota Nation's Sacred Hoop, and that the Sacred Tree was dead.

But in 1973, 83 years after the massacre, at the spot where so many of Big Foot's people had died under fire and amid a snowstorm, there was once again ghost-dancing at Wounded Knee, guided by Leonard Crow Dog and Wallace Black Elk.

In May, 1974 the Ghost Dance was once more revived at Rosebud, directed by old Henry Crow Dog, whose grandfather had been one of the original Ghost Dance leaders. I was invited to document the event, and took my fifteen-year-old daughter, Jackie, along. On the day before the ritual, Leonard Crow Dog told the people: "Only those who want to make a vow to dance for four days without eating or drinking should step into the circle and hold hands." Before I knew what was happening, there was my daughter standing in the circle. "She's only fifteen," I said to Crow Dog. "What if she faints?" "That's my business," he answered. "You just go and take your pictures."

During the night, they made a Ghost Dance shirt and medicine bundle for Jackie and gave her an eagle feather. In the morning, all the dancers got medicine and then went up into the hills where the ground had been prepared. First came the sweat and then the dancing began.

At one point, eagles circled above the dancers. All rejoiced at this good omen. A less welcome bird that also circled above us was an observation plane. Comic relief was provided when the camp *akichita* (camp police) discovered two FBI agents hiding in the bushes, nattily dressed in modern clothes, steadfastly maintaining that they were life insurance salesmen. This was not very smart, since there was not a house within miles nor any likely customers. It seemed that after all those years, the wasichu were still afraid of ghosts.

But there were eagles above, and the songs of birds mingling with the old Ghost Dance songs. Two women fell down in a trance and received visions. Seeing the dancers circling, holding hands, dressed in their ghost shirts and wrapped in upside-down American flags, I felt transported back in time, and half expected the Earth to roll up and the buffalo once more emerge onto the Plains.▷

I'm preparing the sweatlodge for the Ghost Dance. We're bringing it back after all these years. Not the old Ghost Dance, which was supposed to roll up the white's Earth and bring back the Indian Earth underneath, but a new-old spirit. It is like raindrops making a tiny brook, many drops making a stream, many streams making a mighty river bursting all dams. We are the first raindrops.

Henry Crow Dog, May 1974

Henry Crow Dog preparing sweat.

Leroy, ghost-dancer.

This little boy will dance. This young girl will dance. While dancing, your body will be the altar. We'll smoke the pipe; let Mother Earth smoke. The Great Spirit will smoke our smoke. We'll use an eaglebone whistle. Then you'll hear the eagles whistling with us. When you fall down in a trance, then for a while you'll die. You will get into the power. You'll have a good vision. When you come to life again, you'll act as a messenger—relate what you've seen, be a messenger from the ghosts.

Leonard Crow Dog
before the Ghost Dance

"The most sacred thing we have," Lame Deer used to say, "is the Holy Pipe. Its red stone is our flesh and blood. It is our heart. In its bowl is the whole universe. Every grain of tobacco represents a living thing. When you hold the pipe, you can speak nothing but the truth."

George Eagle Elk added, "Whenever you do something spiritual, whenever you want to put on a ceremony, you should first smoke the Pipe. You should use only the right kind of tobacco—*Chanshasha*. Every step—filling the Pipe, smoking it—you should sing the song that goes with it and pray to Tunkashila. You should really light the Pipe with a glowing buffalo chip or, if you can't get hold of one, use a red-hot coal, not a match. You should always pass it to the left, clockwise, because that's how the Sacred Buffalo Woman, Ptesan Win, did it."

Black Elk taught: "When you pray with the Pipe, you pray with and for everything."

John spoke about the Pipe which the White Buffalo Woman had brought to the Sioux: "It is still kept for the tribe by the Looking Horse family at Eagle Butte. It is unlike any other pipe. Its stem is made of a buffalo calf's lower legbone. It is wrapped in buffalo hair and red trade cloth. Eagle feathers and bird skins are tied to it. It is so brittle with age that it can no longer be smoked, but when you touch it you feel power flow into you."

Lame Deer, and other traditional Sioux, say that the Pipe was kept for ten generations by the Elk Head family of the Itaziptcho or "Without Bows" subtribe. They also say that the keepers usually lived to be over a hundred years old. There is an ancient legend telling of a great flood which, long ago, swept over the Plains, crushing all human life beneath its raging waves. The flesh and bones were turned into a large pool of blood. The blood congealed, solidified, and, finally, turned into the Sacred Inyan Sha, the red pipestone used for all the ceremonial pipes. The stone's scientific name is "catlinite" after the painter George Catlin who first described it. It is found in only one quarry in western Minnesota. This quarry was originally on neutral ground, where even enemies could dig the sacred rock peacefully, side by side. Today the quarry has become Pipestone National Monument, and only Indians are allowed to mine and sell catlinite. Old John Lame Deer ended his tales of the Sacred Pipe by describing his feelings as he held the Buffalo Calf Chanunpa (Sacred Pipe): "I held the Pipe. I felt my blood going into the Pipe and felt it coming back. Its spirit entered into my mind. That Pipe was me. I felt it come alive in my hands. Tears were streaming down my face. The Buffalo Pipe made me know myself. It gave me my power." ▷

*Henry Crow Dog
smoking pipe.*

Friend of the Eagle,
To you I pass the pipe first.
Around the circle I pass it to you.
Around the circle to begin the day.
Around the circle I complete the four directions.
I pass the pipe to the Grandfather above.
I smoke with the Great Mystery.
So begins a good day.

Lakota pipe song

Before anything else comes the dream, the crying for a vision, but before a man can go up to the hilltop he must first purify himself in a sweatbath.

Cleansing both body and mind in the sweatlodge was a universal Native American custom. It was practiced by almost every tribe, usually in a religious ceremonial setting. Vapor baths were taken by the Maya and Aztecs long before the arrival of the Spaniards. A sixteenth-century Dominican friar, Diego Durán, described Aztecs taking "dry baths" inside the *temazcalli*, the sweathouses: "These bathhouses are heated with fire and are like small, low huts. Each one can hold ten persons in a squatting position. . . .The entrance is very low and narrow. People enter only one-by-one and on all fours."

There was an Aztec God of the Sweathouse, and during the purification, prayers were chanted. According to the same good friar, the heat engendered was brutal and unbearable: "If a Spaniard were to go through this, he would go into shock and be paralyzed."

Among the Alaskan Inuit (Eskimos), the bathhouse, *kashim*, was a large wooden structure described as the center of religious and social life in each village.

On the American East Coast, an eighteenth-century traveler, visiting the Delawares of Pennsylvania, observed: "In every town an oven situated some distance from the dwellings, built either of stakes or boards, covered with sods, or dug into the side of a hill, and heated with some red-hot stones, is used by them to clean and purify themselves."

The Navajo sweatlodge resembles a small, earth-covered mound with a split-cedar-framed entrance.

Among the Plains Tribes, the sweatlodge ceremony was performed in four intervals amid sacred songs and prayers. In the 1830s, George Catlin painted the picture of a Mandan sweatbath held inside a tipi. The nineteenth-century anthropologist, James Mooney, reported that "among the Kiowa and Cheyenne, the sweatbath is almost a daily custom."

All across America, the "sweat" is practiced in essentially the same way. Pliant sticks are bent and tied together to form a dome four to five feet high, which is covered with blankets. Inside, six to ten people crouch naked around a small pit. The small pit serves as a receptacle for the heated stones, over which cold water is poured to envelop the bathers in hot steam. Depending on the tribe, a sweatbath ceremony may be held upon the arrival of puberty, before going on a hunt or on the warpath, after killing an eagle or human foe, before a sun dance, or for other sacred ceremonies. My sweatlodge photographs were all taken on the Rosebud, South Dakota, Sioux Reservation.

Inikagapi, "taking a sweat," is a rite of purification. It can occasionally be performed just to feel good, clean, and refreshed, or to get rid of all that makes one feel tired or bad, but most often it is a sacred ceremony. As such, it can stand by itself or be the prelude to an even more solemn ritual, such as a vision quest.

In the *inikagapi* we first encounter the rich symbolism inherent in all Indian rituals. As John Collier wrote:

"We have to recognize the role of symbol systems as the conservers and propellers of the deep life of man, the definers and molders of personality, and the pilots of societies in their movement toward half-conscious goals."

The sweatlodge, *inikagapi wokeya*, or *inipi* for short, is made of twelve to sixteen willow sticks planted upright in a circle and bent together at the top to make a beehive-shaped structure. Years ago, this was covered with buffalo skins; today it is covered with tarps or blankets. In the words of Black Elk, spoken half a century ago:

"The sweatlodge utilizes all the powers in the universe, Earth, and the things which grow from earth—water, fire, and air. The water represents the Thunderbeings. . .who bring goodness, and the steam which comes from the rocks, within which is the fire. . .which purifies us so that we may live as Wakan Tanka wills, and he may even send us a vision if we become very pure."

The medicine man, Archie Fire Lame Deer, teaches: "We talk about the twelve uprights and the four horizontals which form the frame of the lodge. Each thing has a symbol and each symbol represents something that is sacred. The ground we pick is a place where there is water nearby, and plenty of wood and, always, the white willow. The willow takes away headaches. It is powerful. My father always told me, 'It's like the bones of the skeleton of our people.' "

Black Elk taught that the willow wands "are to remind us of life and death, because, just as the willow sheds its leaves in winter and renews itself in spring, so people die but live on in the spirit world."

According to Sioux tradition, the sweatlodge, and instructions for how to use it, were brought to the people by Pte-sanwin, the Sacred White Buffalo Woman. Lame Deer teaches that the sweatlodge entrance, no matter what some books say, always faces west "to unite the setting sun with *hanhepi-wi*, the night sun we call the moon. Only the heyoka, the thunder-dreamers, the contraries who do everything different, face their sweatlodge toward east." Black Elk maintained that the *inipi* should face east. There seems to be some difference of opinion.

Lame Deer also teaches that, "one can easily tell a summer from a winter sweatlodge. If the sticks are peeled, it is a summer lodge, for the simple reason that they can easily be stripped during the warm months. A winter lodge is one in which the willow sticks have been left with their bark on." The fire pit in the hut's center, according the Lame Deer, represents the Sun, the great giver of life and energy, while the *inipi* itself stands for Unchi, Grandmother Earth, the Turtle Continent we live on.

The earth taken from the fire pit inside the lodge is used to make a sacred path to a small mound, sometimes referred to as "Unchi," about two feet from the lodge door. A little further is the place called Peta Owihankeshni—the Fire Without End. To construct it, four sticks of wood are laid running east and west, on which are placed four other sticks pointing north and south. Against these lean still more sticks "like a tipi." On top of this wood, the rocks are placed. They represent not only Unchi but also the eternal power of the Grandfather Spirit, "because men die, but the mountains and rocks last forever." Beside the rockpile is usually placed the altar in the shape of a buffalo skull, its eyesockets plugged with sage, the Sacred Pipe resting against one of the horns. There is also a bucket of cold water, not from a tap but from a spring, and a ladle, although sometimes medicine people prefer a bundle of sage, dipped in water, to sprinkle the hot rocks.

Occasionally an ordinary pitchfork is used to pass the rocks inside the lodge, but the right method is to use deer antlers or a forked stick for this purpose. At all stages of preparing the *inipi*, appropriate prayers are said. Before those who want to purify themselves enter the sweatlodge, sage is strewn across the floor.

When I took my first sweatbath over twenty years ago, it was not unusual for men and women to sweat together. Modesty was not offended because all participants came wrapped in towels which they took off only inside the lodge, where it was too dark to see anything. Nowadays men and women sweat separately although the leader running the ceremony is usually an elderly medicine man. When everything has been made *wakan*, holy, the sweaters enter the lodge "sunwise" and sit down on the sage-covered floor. The leader takes his place at the east of the entrance. Outside is the helper who passes the rocks into the hut. He or she also opens and closes the door flap and does everything as the leader directs. The red-hot rocks make a slight crackling sound as they are handed in, one by one. The number of rocks determines how hot the sweat will be. The leader sprinkles sweetgrass over the glowing rocks, and its fragrance quickly fills the little hut. All present wave the smoke toward themselves, rubbing it over their faces and chests. Good spirits are expected to come in at this point, and some mischievous ones also. In the words of Archie Lame Deer: "The Supernaturals bring them in to create problems. They are not really bad. They won't hurt you. They are pranksters. You trip on your own shoe; you sit down because you think there is a chair, but there is no chair. Little things like that."

It is Wakan Tanka whose presence is desired and whose spirit fills the lodge and the minds of all. Prayers are said. Everybody gives thanks to the Creator: "Wakan Tanka, Tunkashila, pilamaye!" Finally, cold water is poured over the hissing rocks. At once, searing white steam fills the hut as a wave of hot air seems to rise from the ground.

A sweat can be a most pleasant and exhilarating experience, but sometimes it can be uncomfortably hot for the unaccustomed wasichu. I remember that once the hot steam curled around my back and gave me a large blister on the left shoulder. Sometimes the air has seemed too hot to be inhaled. I learned to quickly cup my hands over my nose and mouth, creating a space of slightly cooler air, before breathing in. If someone cannot stand the heat, he or she can cry, "*Mitakuye oyasin*— all my relations!" Then the entrance flap is lifted to let cool outside air into the lodge, bringing instant relief. The flap is lifted four times during the ceremony anyway even if nobody asks for it. The pipe is passed around clockwise and every person receiving it says something good or recites a prayer. At last it is finished. One is a little giddy and light-headed from the heat, but also clear-minded and aware of certain powers that are present. One is wonderfully cleaned in body and spirit. As one rubs oneself dry with sage, a great feeling of friendship and harmony unites all those present. The fragrance of sage, sweet-grass, and burning wood lingers for a long time. ▷

Old Henry in sweatlodge.

The Sacred Sweatlodge is your father's home. There is a carpet of sage inside to walk upon. It is made of sweetgrass, the incense of the world that crawls. The lodge frame I make of eighteen willows because it contains the six directions, including up and down, three times. Wood is laid for a fire with four sticks running west and east and seven sticks running north and south. This will allow the spirits to surround the wind. In the meantime, you pray to Grandfather. Look at the fire of life, at *owihankeshni*, the fire without end, as you light up the wood. When the flame has gone down, place twelve round rocks on the glowing coals. They represent twelve eagle feathers. Sprinkle green cedar on the fire for incense. Be blessed by drinking water, the water of life. Pray with the pipe in the six Sacred Directions. Bring the stones with deer antlers into the pit in the center of the lodge. Concentrate your mind. The doorkeeper will pour water over the rocks and the purifying begins. The hot steam enveloping you is Grandfather's breath. Open your pores and your mind!

Crow Dog

GOING
UPON THE HILL

To Native Americans, dreams have an importance unimaginable to the non-Indian. Gods and supernaturals manifest themselves in dreams. Revelations from the spirits reach the supplicant through dreams and visions. Through dreams are conferred magical powers, the gift of prophecy, and the ability to cure illnesses and heal wounds.

Among many tribes it was the common belief that visions had to be earned through fasting and suffering. Hence, for the Sioux, *hanblecheya*, a vision quest, is a "crying" or "lamenting" for a dream. There is often the feeling that, compared to the reality of a dream, the White Man's reality is a mere figment of the imagination, maybe a nightmare.

Generally, a young boy went on his first vision quest at the onset of puberty. He might then receive his grown-up name and a vision of something particularly his own, strictly personal in its power, a "sacred object."

As the Smithsonian's 1910 *Handbook of American Indians* explains: "The Indian painted it on his person or his belongings as a prayer for assistance—a call for help in directing his actions. Any dream of ordinary sleep in which this object appeared had meaning for him and its suggestions were heeded. Men with a natural turn of mind toward the mysterious frequently became shamans and leaders in rites which dealt with the occult. Such persons cultivated their ability to dream and to have visions; the dreams came during natural sleep, the visions during an ecstasy when the man was either wholly or partially unconscious of his surroundings. It was generally believed that such men had power to bring or to avert disaster through direct communication with the unseen."

Dreams revealed to a man whether his medicine was good or not, or whether he should go out on a hunt or stay home. During the Ghost Dance, men and women regularly fell into a trance during which they felt themselves transported to the Moon and the stars. In 1974, I myself, during a revival of the Ghost Dance, observed two women fall down unconscious. After they had reawakened, I listened to them relate visions similar to those of the Ghost Dancers of 1890. Visions that are received during the Sun Dance while the participants are being pierced by or are touching the Sacred Pole, are thought to be of the greatest importance. In some northwestern tribes, to dream about owls constitutes a warning of approaching death, while Sioux believe the elk dreamers receive power to charm women.

To dream of the *wakinyan*, the thunderbirds, according to Frances Densmore, "was considered the greatest honor which could come to a man from a supernatural source, and for this reason the obligation of the dream was heavier than that of any other." (Densmore, p.157)

By this she meant that dreaming of the *wakinyan*, of thunder and lightning, or of any other symbol representing the Thunderbeings, turned a person in a heyoka, a sacred clown or "contrary." Such a man received great power through his dream, power which sometimes frightened the people. As a heyoka, he had to do everything backwards, ride his horse with his face toward its tail, pretend to be shivering with cold in the sweltering heat of summer, or go swimming in icy streams during winter time. The worst was that he had to perform the heyoka *kaga*, the "fool impersonation," in public, no matter how humiliating this might turn out to be. A man having seen himself naked in his thunder dream had to act it out by running through the village without even a breechcloth. According to Pete Catches, a Pine Ridge holy man:

"No matter how shameful his dream, a heyoka has to playact what he dreamt in front of all the people. If he does not do this lightning may kill him. It is very unpleasant to talk about. What I mean, a man that's dreamed about Thunderbeings, right away he's got a fear in him, the fear to perform his act in public the way he dreamt it. I'll tell you a story about a heyoka who acted out his vision. I saw this back in the 1920's. And this man was really lively. He turned somersaults and there was a bunch of young cowboys chasing him on horseback and they could not catch up to him. He was running in front of them, from time to time turning somersaults, and sometimes he was running backwards, and whenever they got close he always managed to get away from them. They tried to lasso him and they couldn't do it. When he was through and undressed I saw that he was an old man in his seventies and yet he had outrun those cowboys on their fast horses. So that's something the people dread to dream about."

In spite of the powers received by a thunder dreamer, many heyokas wished to be their own normal selves again. In order to cease being a contrary, a man had to undergo a certain dogfeast ritual put on by his fellow clowns. During this ritual he had to fish the dog's head out of boiling kettle of dog soup. Pete Catches comments:

"They say it's fantastic, or ridiculous, but it is so. There'll be a pot of boiling water that's bubbling up and down like that. They'll butcher a dog and cook it. At the precise moment, he would run up there, put this whole arm into that boiling pot, search around in there, and get the head. He would run with this, give it to a certain person, and he dreams this before, to which man or woman he would give the head, and this person would just about be scalded. That person would throw it to another man and he would get burned. Five or six would throw it, because they couldn't hold it."

Frances Densmore, among whose informants were many old men who had experienced the heady, free-roaming, pre-reservation days, wrote this about the importance of dreams among the Lakotas:

"The obligation of a dream was as binding as the necessity of fulfilling a vow, and disregard of either was said to be punished by the forces of nature, usually by a stroke of lightning. Dreams were sought by the Sioux but it was recognized that the dream would correspond to the character of the man. Thus it was said that 'a young man would not be great in mind and so his dream would not be like that of a chief; it would be ordinary in kind, yet he would have to do whatever the dream directed him to do'. . . .If the dream were connected with the Sacred Stones, or with herbs or animals connected with the treatment of the sick, it was considered obligatory that the man avail himself of the supernatural aid vouchsafed him in the dream, and arrange his life in accordance with it." (Densmore, p.157)

The most solemn ritual connected with dreams is the vision quest. It involves "going upon the hill" to one's sacred place, and fasting and praying alone there for four days and nights, "crying for a vision." In some cases a man might do this by simply leaning naked, except for a loincloth, against a tree or rock on a lonely hilltop. I once witnessed a *hanblecheya* on the hill of an old holy man, Bill Eagle Feathers. His hill was a badlands-type butte which had served as his "dreaming spot" for many years. This lonely, windswept hill was covered with many sacred things—colored flags, tobacco and cloth offerings, herb bundles, oddly shaped rocks and pebbles, and the skulls of various animals. Other families or individuals have vision pits in which to pray for enlightenment.

The first vision quest I photographed occurred in 1967 at Rosebud on the dreaming hill of the Crow Dog family. The vision seeker was a middle-aged man, a relative of the Crow Dogs, who had fasted many times before. He told me that he had a problem which he hoped a vision would solve for him. At the foot of the hill stood his sister-in-law making a flesh offering, *cheh'pi wanunyanpi*. This flesh offering involved the dreamer's wife cutting 50 tiny squares of skin from her sister's arms. These were carefully put, one by one, on tissue paper, and later into a softly rattling gourd. This he was to take with him to the hilltop. Its sound was meant to comfort him during his long ordeal—a reminder that someone had undergone pain to help him in his quest.

After a ceremonial sweat, friends and relatives accompanied the "lamenter" to the vision pit atop the pine-studded butte. The pit was L-shaped, consisting of a hip-deep vertical shaft and, at its bottom, a horizontal chamber into which the man crawled, taking only the gourd, a sacred pipe, and a small bag of native tobacco. Over the pit was spread a large tarpaulin which, in turn, was covered with earth. It almost seemed as if the man were being buried alive. It brought to my mind what Pete Catches had told me:

"A man going to the hilltop for a *hanblecheya* gives his flesh and bones to the Great Spirit. And if he is accepted, he goes on living, but his soul, his ghost, his spirit is working apart from his body. He has been given a power. It is almost like dying, only you come back from this death. That's a hard thing to do."

After the pit had been smoothed over with earth, tobacco offerings laid out in a square, and four colored flags, representing the four directions, had been put up, everybody left, leaving the vision seeker entombed in his pit. Four days later they returned to "bring him back to life again." I thought that it took a lot of courage and stamina to undergo a vision quest in this severe manner. Women also "go upon the hill," but in their case the fasting is done in the open, not in a pit, and limited to two days and nights. There is a well-documented case of one man who fasted a full sixteen days—a superhuman feat.

Old John Lame Deer remembered his first vision quest and told me about it:

"I felt the spirits of my long dead forefathers entering my body, felt them stirring in my mind and in my heart. Sounds came to me through the darkness: the cries of the winds, the whisper of trees, the hooting of birds. Suddenly I felt an overwhelming presence. Down there with me in my cramped hole was a big bird. The pit was only as wide as myself and I was a skinny boy, but that huge bird was flying around me as if he had the whole sky to himself. I could hear his cries, sometimes near and sometimes far away. I felt his wings touching me. This feeling was so overwhelming that it was just too much for me. I trembled and my bones turned to ice. I grasped the rattle with the forty pieces of my grandmother's flesh. I shook it and it made a soothing sound, like rain falling on a rock. I took the Sacred Pipe in my other hand and started to sing and pray: 'Tunkashila, Grandfather, help me!' I was no longer myself. I started to cry. Crying, even my voice was different. I sounded like an old man. I couldn't even recognize this strange voice. I used long-ago words in my prayer, words no longer used today. I tried to wipe away my tears, but they wouldn't stop. In the end I just pulled that star quilt over me, rolled myself up in it.

"Then I heard a human voice, strange and high-pitched, which could not come from an ordinary being. All at once I was up there with the birds. I could look down, even on the stars, and the Moon was close to my left side. The voice spoke: 'You are sacrificing yourself here to become a medicine man. In time you will be one. We are the fowl nation, the winged ones, the eagles. You shall be our brother. You are going to understand us whenever you come up here to seek a vision.' I felt that these voices were good, and slowly my fear left me. I had lost all sense of time. I didn't know whether it was night or day. I was asleep, yet wide awake. Then I saw a shape before me. It rose from the darkness and the swirling fog which penetrated my earth hole. I saw that this was my great-grandfather, Tah'ca Ushte, Lame Deer, Old Man Chief of the Minneconjou. I understood that he wished me to take his name. This made me glad beyond words. Again I wept. This time with happiness.

"I don't know how long I had been up there, one minute or a lifetime. I felt a hand on my shoulder gently shaking me. It was Uncle Chest who had come for me. 'You have been up here for four days, hokshila,' he told me. 'Time to come down.' I was to tell him everything that had happened to me and he would interpret my visions so that I could understand what they meant. He told me also that I was no longer a boy, that I was a man now. I was Lame Deer." ▷

Crying for a vision, that's the beginning of all religion. The thirst for a dream from above, without this you are nothing. This I believe. It is like the prophets in your bible, like Jesus fasting in the desert, getting his visions. It's like our Sioux vision quest, the *hanblecheya*. White men have forgotten this. God no longer speaks to them from a burning bush. If he did, they wouldn't believe it, and call it science fiction.

Your old prophets went into the desert crying for a dream and the desert gave it to them. But the white men of today have made a desert of their religion and a desert within themselves. The White Man's desert is a place without dreams or life. There nothing grows. But the spirit water is always way down there to make the desert green again.

Lame Deer, 1970

Leonard Crow Dog in vision pit.

LITTLE LIGHTS
IN THE DARK

The strangest of all Sioux rituals is the *yuwipi* ceremony, during which the medicine man, the "stone dreamer," is wrapped in a star blanket, tied completely around with a rawhide thong, and laid face down on the floor, looking like a mummy about to be buried. The outsider witnessing such a ritual is usually so fascinated by this "mummifying" aspect that he or she remains unaware that the *yuwipi* is basically a Sacred Stone rite.

The idea of stones having mysterious powers, and even life, is not uniquely Indian. Excavations in the Magdalenian caves of France have yielded oddly shaped, painted pebbles which are obviously charms and talismans or, in Native American terms, "medicine." Certain rocks have been worshipped as sacred by peoples throughout the world. The Celts had their ogham stones, their drumlechs or enchanted rock circles, their menhirs, dolmen, and Stonehenges. The Scandinavians had their runic stones. The Romans used lapis lazuli in their rainmaking ceremonies. In India, barren women venerated and adorned themselves with stone lingams. In both Europe and Asia, precious stones were worshipped as the embodiment of gods, worn as amulets and love charms, or used to foretell the future. Even today, healing with crystals has become popular. Meso-Americans prayed to the jade god and used jade to cure diseases of the kidneys. Both Lord Roseberry and Lord Rothschild supposedly wore jade talismans to help their racehorses win the Derby.

For the Sioux, the words *tunka* and *inyan* (both mean "rock") hold special sacred meanings. *Tunka* was the Lakota's oldest god, representing the Creator's eternal nature: "Everything has a birth and death, but Tunka has no birth and death." Also: "Tunka is the spirit who fell from the sky. He is a rock. He knows all secrets. He finds that which is lost." The word *tunka* reoccurs in Tunkashila, an alternate name for Wakan Tanka, the Everywhere Spirit. *Tunka yatapika* represents the glowing rock inside the sweatlodge wherein the Creator's spirit dwells.

Inyan, a term less ancient than *tunka*, is sometimes referred to as "Grandfather Rock," while *Inyan-Sha*, or red stone, is the name for the sacred catlinite pipestone, the "flesh and blood of the Indian." Sioux legends tell of their culture hero, Inyan Hokshi, the Stone Boy, slayer of the monster witch, whose mother gave birth to him after having been made pregnant by a pebble she swallowed.

When the White Buffalo Woman came to the people, she brought to them not only the Sacred Pipe but also drew from her medicine bundle a perfectly round, very *wakan* stone. Such holy stones are still carried by some traditional Sioux as their *wotawe* or charm. Crazy Horse wore such a round pebble behind his ear which, people said, made him bullet proof.

Lame Deer explained: "Such a stone is round like the universe. Like Wakan Tanka, it has no beginning and no end. Great power dwells within it. Such stones make holy talk."

Brave Buffalo, interviewed by Frances Densmore, said: "These stones are round, like the Sun and the Moon, and we know that all things which are round are related to each other. . .These stones have lain there a long time looking at the Sun. . .The Thunderbird is said to be related to these stones. . .In all my life I have been faithful to the Sacred Stones. I have lived according to their requirements: they have helped me in all my troubles." (Densmore, p. 208)

Lame Deer pointed out whitish rocks to me that had spidery cracks containing traces of green moss. "These are like books," he said, "containing writing for those who have the power to read it. In these rocks is *sichun*, power." He also told me of "finding stones" used by medicine men to locate buffalo or lost articles. He also picked up tiny crystalline rocks from anthills, explaining, "We use these *yuwipi wasichu* to put into *wagmuha* (rattles) during the *yuwipi* ceremony. These little shiny rocks have power, and so have the ants who collect them for us."

The *yuwipi* ceremony has been called "the only ancient cult still practiced among the modern Sioux." The Sun Dance and the vision quest may be equally ancient. That the *yuwipi* ritual goes far back in time is beyond question. Early travelers described rites resembling *yuwipi*, such as a shaman making stones fly around in a darkened tipi. A Jesuit father described such objects as "devilish stones which Satan hurls at those who do not believe in his existence."

Father Eugene Buechel's comprehensive Lakota dictionary defines *yuwipi* as "transparent stones, usually found on anthills and used in the *wakan wichoh'an* called *yuwipi*, which consists in one being tied all round and being loosed by magic." *Yuwi* he translated as "to wrap around, bind up," and *yuwipi wasichu* as "a sacred round stone that is supposed to have power in the hands of those who have dreamed." The stones, the wrapping, and the tying up are thus connected in language.

Rituals that combine being tied up, finding objects, and diagnosing illnesses are not exclusively Sioux. The Danish explorer, Peter Freuchen, described a ceremony, performed in an igloo, which closely resembles *yuwipi*:

"Then Krilerneq took several sealskin lines and bound Sorqaq tight, tying his arms to his body and binding his legs together. . . . Next, Krilerneq joined the audience and put out the lamps, except for one tiny flame; the light was so faint that we could barely see each other's faces.

"There was loud drumming and singing, getting stronger and stronger. . . . Suddenly Krilerneq put on the lights. Sorqaq had disappeared. . . he was definitely gone. I looked around at the audience, and I could hardly recognize the calm quiet friends who had come down to us to trade. Their faces were ecstatic, their eyes bright and unseeing. Naked from the waist up, they swayed back and forth to the rhythm of the song. . . .

"The song continued and tore me along with it. I lost all sense of time and place. . ." Freuchen was told that the *angakok* (medicine man) had trouble returning from the spirit lands. At last "the performance was over, and all the lamps in the igloo were lit. Sorqaq was sitting on the ledge, strapped tightly in his sealskin lines. . ." (Freuchen, p. 226-229)

As in a *yuwipi* ceremony, things had taken place which could not be explained by the White Man's logic. Freuchen wrote: "My point of view has always been that there is nothing supernatural, only things for which we so far have no scientific explanation. So I just relate what I saw and heard, and I have heard other people—wiser and more sober-minded than I—recount similar experiences."

Stephen Feraca, a long-time official of the Bureau of Indian Affairs who by no stretch of the imagination can be called visionary or gullible, wrote about a *yuwipi* man called Horn Chips who could speak in several voices at the same time and who, in order to test his powers, was challenged to perform the ritual in a lighted room with the Indian Police doing the tying up. The *yuwipi* lights flashed all over the ceiling for everyone to see as Horn Chips' powers were evident to all present.

Frances Densmore described one *yuwipi* curing ceremony which took place over a hundred years ago, held in a darkened tent, during which the medicine man spoke in the voices of animals, gave an impression of buffalo coming into the tent, had objects flying through the air, and was finally revealed in the light of a grass fire being wedged, untied, between the poles near the top of the lodge.

Another ritual, also described by Densmore, goes back even further. It was related to her by an old Sioux, Lone Man, at the turn of the century:

Once a war party had been gone two months; no news of them had been received, and it was feared that all had been killed. In their anxiety the people appealed to Bear Necklace, asking him to ascertain, by means of the sacred stones, what had become of the war party. Bear Necklace requested them to bind his arms behind him, then to tie his fingers and toes, interlacing them with twisted sinew. He was then wrapped in a buffalo robe and tied with ropes. His medicine drum, medicine bag, and a bell were hung high on the tent poles, and he was laid on the ground beneath them. The tent was darkened, he sang his song and told his dreams. The tent then began to tremble, the articles hanging from the pole dropped to the ground, his cords loosened, and he stood entirely free. As soon as the medicine articles fell to the ground, there appeared a row of four or five small round stones ready to tell him what he wanted to know. Bear Necklace then gave correct information concerning the absent war party. . . . Afterwards the stones always told him the names of those who were killed in war, the names of the survivors, and the day on which they would return. This information was always correct.

I myself have observed more than a dozen *yuwipi* ceremonies. Among the *yuwipi* men at whose rites I have been present were John Strike, who made innumerable lights flicker across the ceiling of his humble log cabin; George Eagle Elk, who performed the ceremony in a lighted room; Godfrey Chips, a stone dreamer only fourteen years old at the time; and Leonard Crow Dog who, besides being a *yuwipi* man, also directs ghost and sun dances as well as meetings of the Peyote Church.

A person who wants help usually sends a pipe to the *yuwipi* man, who never accepts payment for his services. It is, however, expected that the "sponsor" will feed all who come to participate. The participants, on their part, are each required to eat at least one morsel of dog meat, because *yuwipi* is also a dog feast. I end the description of *yuwipi* with a verse from the Stone Dreamer's song:

> In the direction of the sunset
> the wind is blowing
> and these stones
> one round, another round
> flying,
> continuing to fly,
> behold them!

As to the impossibility of explaining to myself, or to my friends, the "unexplainable" in *yuwipi* ritual, I can only quote Fiona McLeod:

"In the lost Eden of the human heart, an ancient tree of knowledge grows wherefrom the mind has not yet gathered more than a few windfalls." (Collier, p. 80) ▷

Yuwipi ceremony, Rosebud Sioux Reservation, South Dakota.

The tying up, the thongs, the string of tobacco ties have a deep meaning for us. This is tying us together, ending the isolation between one human being and another; it is making a line from man to the Great Spirit. It means a harnessing of power. The man is tied up so that the spirits can come and use him. It pulls the people together and teaches them.

Lame Deer, Minneconjou Sioux

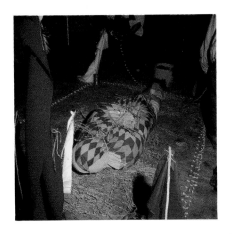

Yuwipi is a finding-out ritual. It is a ceremony of *inyan*, of *tunka*—the rock, the stone. It is a dogfeast. It is a rite of tiny crystal rocks gathered by the ants and put into gourds, a rite of flickering lights, of the star blanket, the eagle feather and the deer tail, a rite of ghostly voices. It is a mystery.

Bill Eaglefeathers

Little Ina with Buffalo Skull. Healing ceremony.

This is a healing ceremony. A child is going to be healed. You can heal one who is sick with the power of herbs or with the power of the spirit, the power of the eagle wing, the smoldering cedar, the sage. You can use certain stones for healing because they, too, have power. You can use the power of an animal—the buffalo, the coyote, the eagle, the bear, the elk. There are many ways of healing known to the *pejuta wichasha* (medicine man).

Henry Crow Dog

In addition to the Ghost Dance, there is another religion which came to the Sioux from the outside. This is the Peyote Cult, also known as the "Native American Church." The word peyote derives from the Aztec *peyotl*, meaning caterpillar, because of the fuzziness of the "button." Among the Lakota, it is known either as *unchela*, or simply as *pejuta*—medicine. Peyote is a small cactus which grows chiefly in the dry country of southern Texas, along the Rio Grande, and below the border in Mexico where the peyote cult is widespread among the Tarahumara, Huichols, and Yaquis. Peyote was already known to the Spanish priests who accompanied the conquistadores. They called it the "devil's root" because it was "used in hellish rites of sorcery, intoxicating the Indians and keeping them from salvation." It was "an abomination" because it violated Church doctrine which forbade prophesying: "This plant enables the Chichimecas who eat it to look into the future, foreseeing if an enemy will attack them or if the weather will continue fair, and other things of that nature."

Peyote was unknown north of the border until the middle of the nineteenth century. The man who did the most to introduce the Peyote Cult to the North American tribes was Quanah Parker, a Comanche chief. He was the son of Nokoni, the Wanderer, a warlike Comanche headman, and a white mother, Cynthia Ann Parker, whom his father had abducted during a raid when Cynthia was about twelve years old. She was eventually rescued by white soldiers and returned to Texas, while Quanah remained with the tribe. He grew up to be a fierce warrior and, in 1874, was a leader in the famous Battle of Adobe Walls. Recognizing early that resistance to the whites was useless, he made peace and led his people into a quiet existence of farming and husbandry.

After his mother died, the Parker family invited Quanah to come to Texas where they would teach him farming and ranching. He fell seriously ill and his life was despaired of. White doctors could not help him, and he asked for an Indian medicine man. Grandmother Parker could not produce one, but found a substitute—a half Mexican, half Tarahumara, "curandera" or "bruja," a woman wise in the use of herbs, who cured Quanah with peyote. Thus he was introduced to the Sacred Herb and brought it to his people. It helped that the Comanches were southwestern Indians, close to the only area where peyote could be found inside the United States, referred to by modern Sioux as their "peyote garden."

As taught by Quanah Parker, the peyote religion was a blend of native and Christian beliefs. A sympathetic anthropologist, James Mooney, helped Quanah to organize and incorporate the new religion under the name, Native American Church. Like the Ghost Dance, the peyote religion was born of despair, helping the poor full-bloods forget hunger and oppression, lifting up the hearts of their women. It soon spread from the tribe to tribe, sinking deep roots among the Kiowa and Comanche, the Navajo and Apache, the Arapaho, Crows, and Cheyenne. It came to the Sioux comparatively late, sometime around 1920. At Rosebud, Henry Crow Dog was among the first to practice the Peyote Cult.

Leaders of the Native American Church maintain that, among some 35,000 Sioux, fully one-third are full-time or part-time participants in peyote meetings. These meetings are now also taking place in Indian communities in Los Angeles, Minneapolis, Denver, Chicago, and Rapid City. The Native American Church has attracted many young non-Indians to the reservations, and there are groups of whites practicing the peyote religion in various forms.

The missionaries did not take kindly to the new faith, calling peyote a barrier to civilization, "Satan's fruit," or a "deadly drug." It was therefore outlawed and suppressed. The fight against the "fiendish plant" was led by a weird character called "Pussyfoot" Johnson, a U.S. Marshal six days a week, and on Sundays a hellfire and brimstone evangelist, who, between 1904 and 1920, used to deliver subpoenas for drinking and ingesting peyote in his tailcoat and top hat.

Contrary to what its enemies say, peyote is not addictive. It is mild in its effects, and leaves no hangover. According to the *Handbook of American Indians* of 1910:

"Tests so far made indicate that it [peyote] possesses varied and valuable medicinal properties, tending to confirm the idea of the Indians who regard it almost as a panacea. . . . The drug produces a sort of spiritual exaltation differing entirely from that produced by any other known drug, and apparently without any reaction."

I myself have participated in about a dozen peyote meetings in strictly spiritual settings. With one exception, the effect was always mild, making me contemplative, and inducing a slightly trance-like state, more the result of the hypnotizing throb of the water drum than of the "medicine." Peyote is taken in the form of dried buttons, chopped–up mush, or even as tea. Its earth-like taste can be unpleasant. It makes some people gag and vomit. This is considered part of "taking the sacrament" and disturbs no one. For those who need it, there is always a large, empty, tin can handy.

Meetings are ritualistically regulated. As the good Christian goes to church on Sunday, so members of the Native American Church have their meetings every Saturday night, lasting from sundown to sunup. The ceremony is run by the road chief, who guides the participants on the path to life. He is assisted by the fire chief, who watches over the glowing embers, the cedar chief, who sprinkles fragrant cedar powder over the flames, the door keeper, and the drummer. There is always a woman who brings in the morning water. When I first witnessed meetings, they had a strong Christian flavor—an open bible, readings from the book of Revelation, and peyote songs with English words, such as "Jesus, Light of the World; Jesus, Sun of the World," or, in Lakota:

> Jazuz, onshimalaye.
> Nita Canku wanjayanke makiye lo.
> Hay nay Yowai.
>
> Jesus, pity me.
> Lead me on your road.

Since the comeback of Indian religion, the Christian element has faded, and instead of the bible, the Sacred Pipe is much in evidence. A meeting can be run Plains style or Southern style. In the words of Crow Dog:

"The Native American Church of the South, they call it the Half Moon Way. They use cornhusk cigarettes. They use Bull Durham while we Sioux use cedar. They eat the whole button, don't make the medicine into a mush. Like us they use the staff, sage, whistle, and drum, and they put the chief peyote, the one they are going to partake, at the altar. They make the altar in the shape of a big half moon. They make it of white sand with red earth on the bottom, and a little trail on top of the altar."

Peyote has become a pan-Indian, intertribal affair, with people borrowing songs and variations of ritual from other tribes.

Peyote has its own symbolism. The Native American Church's main symbol is the Water Bird, which is seen again and again in silver jewelry worn by "peyoters." Participants often wear prayer shawls, half red and half blue. Paraphernalia consists of the staff, the feather fan, the gourd rattle, the water drum, and the bone whistle.

During the night, the peyote goes around four times, so everybody takes four buttons or spoonfuls. I have seen one road man take as many as seventy buttons, "getting into the power" but never getting out of control. The paraphernalia goes around clockwise from person to person, and everybody has the privilege of singing when the staff and the gourd reach him or her—usually four songs at a time. A meeting ends in the morning with food and coffee, friendly talk, good feelings, and being pleasantly tired. Crow Dog described to me the ceremony's etiquette and meaning:

"Grandfather Peyote, he has no ears, but he listens. He has no mouth, but he talks to you. He has no eyes, but he sees into your heart. Before sunset everybody stands before the tipi. The cedar man says a prayer. Everybody follows the road man into the tipi. You should stay put in your place all through, but when nature calls you may go out, but don't go in front of the person who is taking medicine. So they sing sixteen songs, four rounds. Starting songs, they call it, then midnight songs. There's a water call before they say any prayer. The fire chief takes cedar and smokes the water. As the water goes around, the road man asks everybody to say something good. After the water gets through, when it gets back to the door man, the speaker sits down. The big pause comes at midnight—midnight water. The third round is toward the morning. After each round there is a pause. Any new-comer you have among you, give him the cedar. Maybe he needs it. The road man asks the newcomer to come to the fire and prays for him. He fans him from the four directions with the eaglefeather. Then he cedars everybody. Then come the morning songs.

"The first song is: 'Great Spirit, bless my people. Take care of the coming generation. Bless the universe.' The second song is: 'Bless all relatives, the dead ones too.' The third song is at water call: 'Bless all the waters.' The fourth song is for all tribes: 'The wind of the echoes, blessing from the West, bless all Ikce Wichasha (the natural people, that is, the Sioux).'

"Then they bring in the morning food—corn, jerk meat, *wasna* of two kinds (pemmican), sweet choke cherries, coffee. Then the road man looks around for someone mourning or from far away; he lets them drink the water first. The cedar man blesses the fire and all stretch out their hands over the flames.

"The road man explains about the peyote. Peyote is a little old man sitting at the altar. The White Man goes to the Moon, but the Indian was already there, spiritually, with the Sacred Herb and the peyote gets him safely back. After eating, the first man who drank the water says: 'Good Morning.' That's it."

In all the meetings I participated in, I hallucinated only once. I had to fly back to New York on a Saturday at noon, so my friends insisted on having a special meeting for me the Friday before. I took no more peyote than on other occasions—actually less—but suddenly my speech became slurred, my movements unsteady, my hearing acute, and my eyes saw everything around me in golden, glowing colors. I also forgot all my songs except one. And I was befriended by a red horse. I saw it, I smelled it, I heard it nickering. After morning water, I had to drive ninety miles to Pierre in order to catch my plane, but always there was the red horse in front of my rented car. I knew it was not really there, but still I stepped on the brake or "drove around it."

Finally I opened the door and the horse climbed in with me. It also flew with me. Once on the plane, all the forgotten peyote songs came back to me and I began to sing them, to the astonishment of my fellow passengers. The moment the plane touched down at La Guardia, I stopped singing, the red horse disappeared, and the magic was gone. New York will do this to you. ▷

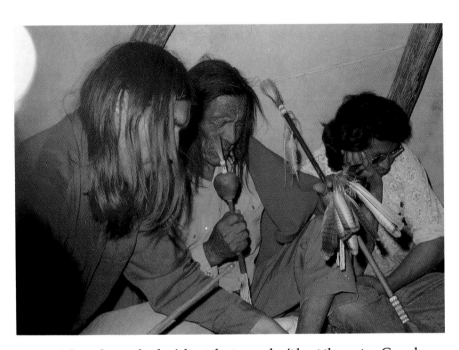

Henry Crow Dog performing a peyote ritual, 1975

Don't hurt the earth, don't hurt the trees, don't hurt the water. Grandfather Peyote, he came right out from this earth, a little plant, talking to that woman who found him, calling out to her, "Come, eat me! Get some earth wisdom!" Long ago the water drum was no brass kettle. Long ago the hide was buffalo skin. Now it's moose. The hide is Jesus' skin as he was beaten by the soldiers. It's Indian skin beaten by some policeman. The hide is all the four-leggeds who have given us food. The drumstick is the stick they whipped Jesus with, the stick the government uses on Mister Indian. It is carved from cedar. It stands for the trees and all the green things. The feather fan, that's for catching good songs out of the air. The gourd rattle, the head, the gourd—that's the Indian's skull, full inside after eating medicine. The staff, that's the staff of authority. Thoughts come down that stick from the spirit; songs go up that stick from the man. You look at all the things we use in a meeting and have a lot to think about.

Road man Carl Iron Shell
of the Native American Church, 1967

A Sound
Of Eaglebone
Whistles

The Sun Dance is the most solemn and important ritual of the Plains Indians, the "Granddaddy of them all," as Pete Catches puts it. The dance is common to many Plains tribes such as the Lakota, Arapaho, Cheyennes, Assiniboins, Crows, Kiowas, Poncas, Shoshoni, and Utes. Closely related to it is the Mandans' Okipa ritual, painted by Bodmer and Catlin in the 1830s. For some of the tribes, the Mandans and Sioux for instance, the dance involves "piercing," a form of self-torture. This aspect has been often misunderstood by whites, who thought that it was an initiation into the tribe, or a way to prove one's courage. As Lame Deer explained:

"During a vision quest, a man sits alone by himself on a hilltop, having his private communion with Wakan Tanka. The Sun Dance is *all* the people communicating with *all* the spirit powers. It is the *hanblecheya* of the whole Sioux Nation. It is not a macho dance to show how much you can endure. It is a prayer and a sacrifice. One takes part in it in obedience to a vow."

It has been said that the Sun Dance was at the center of a tribe's existence, "the opportunity for the expression of emotion in rhythm." Mari Sandoz, who grew up close to the Sioux, had her own, poetic interpretation for the custom of piercing:

"To the old buffalo hunters uninfluenced by Christian symbolism...the ceremonial was based on the idea that all things come forth in travail. It was so with the buffalo cow producing the yellow calf, the earth breaking as the grass bursts forth, the clouds splitting for the rain. Even the tree bled as the bow was cut and the stone as the arrowhead was shaped from its heart."

A person would make a vow to dance in order to take away sickness from a friend or relative, or to bring a warrior back alive from a battle. A man might want to suffer so that the tribe would live. Viewed by government agents and missionaries, the Sun Dance was a savage, bloodthirsty rite which had to be suppressed. And so, in the face of the Constitution's guarantee of religious freedom for all, the Sun Dance and all other Native American rituals were outlawed in 1881. Even taking a sweatbath became a punishable offense. In his 1882 report, McGillicudy, the agent at Pine Ridge wrote: "The heathenish annual ceremony termed 'the Sun Dance' will, I trust, soon be a thing of the past." He was wrong.

The Sun Dance simply went underground. It was finally permitted again during the administration of Franklin D. Roosevelt, "without self-torture," at the insistence of the missionaries. Mari Sandoz, in her little gem of a book, *These were the Sioux*, recalled a touching, evocative scene:

"Several of us interested in the Sioux were there to watch the head dancer, seventy-eight [years old], lean and gaunt as any of the buffalo-hunting followers of Crazy Horse out on the Powder River. Dusty in his paint and flapping breechcloth, the old dancer made his slow little jumping, slipping steps, always turned to face the broiling sun as the drummers pounded the green calfskin, the voices of the singers rising and gone, to rise again.... On the final afternoon he was beginning to move in a curious trance-like flow, almost without steps. Suddenly he stopped, cried out in a thin high falsetto, gesturing to his bare breast, crying to the sky and the Sun Dance Pole and all around.

" 'He wants the thongs,' a uniformed Indian policeman told us, as voices from the headmen replied to the dancer, patient at first, then angrily and with a denying tone, firm. It could not be allowed.

" 'Not allowed!' An old woman near us exclaimed, the words plainly unfamiliar upon her tongue but their meaning sudden and dark.

"For a moment the lean old dancer hung as from a string that did not exist. Then he crumpled into the dust. A murmur of horror swept the crowd, the eagle-wing fans still . . .

"After a while word spread that the old dancer was alive, sleeping, his four-day ordeal cut short, finished. But there would be bronco busting at the rodeo corrals, beginning immediately. The riding was good, and it seemed that almost no one remembered, or even knew, that at the Sun Dance Pole an old man's moment of hope and belief had come and gone." (Sandoz, p.113-115)

When I witnessed my first Sun Dance, in 1967, men were piercing again, but somewhat timidly, through a piece of skin over the left breast. Pete Catches was dancing, a dozen eagle feathers imbedded in his flesh which, he said, hurt more than the actual piercing. Today, men are again hanging from the Sun Dance Pole as shown in the old Bodmer and Catlin paintings. Dancers are again dragging up to twelve buffalo skulls fastened to skewers in their backs. One time Leonard Crow Dog was pierced in four places, front and back, the rawhide ropes attached to four horses which were driven off toward the four directions of the universe.

In 1977 I watched a young man, obviously one whom the Sioux call a *winkte* (homosexual), pierced in four places, the thongs attached to four poles enclosing him. This was the hardest way, because he could not tear himself loose with a sudden pull or backwards leap.

With languid movements and a dreamlike expression on his face, the young man, swaying gently back and forth, took a long time working himself free.

One curious aspect of the modern Sun Dance is that Native Americans come to participate from many tribes which had never practiced this ritual in previous centuries. I have watched Ojibways, Iroquois, Menominees, a lone Apache, even a Mexican Huichol being pierced. In some cases these were big-city Indians from tribes whose languages and ceremonies had become virtually extinct. It was as if, by sun-dancing with the Sioux, they were trying to reclaim something they had lost.

One thing that is no longer seen is the old-time dance lodge, 60 to 100 hundred feet in diameter, resembling a wooden tipi made of upright and slanting poles. Instead, there is now the open Sun Dance "shade" where the spectators can sit, protected from the sun by a circle of pine boughs.

As with all Lakota rituals, the Sun Dance has its own symbols: the camp circle represents the universe, the altar the essence of life, the buffalo skull the people's close relationship to this holy animal. The small figures of a man and a bison, made of buffalo hide and hanging from the pole, and formerly endowed with exaggerated male parts, stand for fertility, the increase of both humans and animals. The crotch of the cottonwood tree is the symbolic nest of the Thunderbirds, while the pole itself is the Tree of Life. Reaching into the clouds, the pole connects Earth with sky, and the people with the Grandfather Spirit above.

The ceremony is always held in midsummer when, as Henry Crow Dog said, "the grass is high, the land green, the choke cherries ripe, the minds of young men and women turn to love, when both humans and the four-legged are happy."

The *wiwanyank wachipi*, literally "looking at the Sun Dance," is directed by the dance chief, *itanchan*, and the intercessor, *kuwá kiyápi*. Four young men, known for their integrity, are sent out as scouts to find the perfect *chan wakan*, the cottonwood tree to be used as the center pole.

"The young men went out on horseback," says Lame Deer, "armed and dressed as for war, because the tree was an enemy to be captured. When the scouts had found the right one they raced back to camp and reported it to the dance leaders. The next morning all the people rode out, men and women in their best beaded and quilled outfits, some warriors with black face paint singing brave heart songs, because, as I said, the tree was an enemy to be conquered. The young men counted coup upon it as in war.

"Four specially chosen women cut the tree down. They were maidens who had never been with a man. If one of them had lied about this, then the boy who had slept with her would have made this known at once, to her shame. But this never happened."

As the tree falls, it is caught by the bearers who will carry it to the dance circle. It is not allowed to touch the ground. In the center of the dancing place, a hole is dug and buffalo fat is put in it. The tree is planted in this hole while the pole-raising song is intoned. Speaking in the name of the pole, the people sing:

> I am standing
> At the Earth's center.
> In a sacred manner
> I see the tribe
> Gathered around me.
> Behold me.

Offerings of tobacco bundles and colored cloth are tied to the pole. The drummers use their sticks. They begin to sing: "Wakan Tanka, Tunkashila, onshimalaye"—"Great Spirit, Grandfather, pity me." The dance begins.

The dancers wear long kilts, mostly red, though some are blue or white. They are naked from the waist up, barefooted, their long hair hanging loose. Not a few have their faces painted. All wear medicine bundles on their chests, and wreaths of sage on their heads and around their wrists. Clenched between their teeth are plumed and quilled eaglebone whistles. Dancing, looking at the Sun, the men blow rhythmically on their whistles, making the sound of a hundred birds. They dance from sun-up to sunset. At certain intervals they sit down and rest for a short while, but are not allowed to eat or drink. If, however, one of the dancers should grow faint with thirst, a relative is allowed to dip a bundle of sage into water and use it to moisten his lips.

The dance lasts four days. On the afternoon of the last day, the piercing takes place. I have watched Lame Deer, Eagle Feathers, Crow Dog, Fools Crow, and Catches doing the piercing. These days, most dancers are pierced in two places on their chests. Women are also now being pierced, mostly on their wrists, and sometimes at their collar bones. Lame Deer always used an ordinary pocket knife so deftly and quickly that many dancers preferred to be pierced by him. Others commented with a wry smile that Eagle Feathers took his time sawing back and forth: "If you ever have a mind to be pierced, pick anybody but Bill."

A sharpened wooden skewer, or more seldom an eagle claw, is passed through the wound and attached to the rawhide thongs dangling from the pole. The dancer later gives these skewers to his friends for tamping down the tobacco in their Sacred Pipes. Attached to the tree, the men dance forwards and backwards, at times so far back that the skin on their breasts is stretched to the breaking point. Friends and relatives encourage the dancers. If one of them drags buffalo skulls around the circle, his friends walk beside him and, if the skulls do not break through, they grab him under the arms and hurry him along. They may even have little children ride on the skulls to make them heavier, so that they are sure to come loose. Likewise, if a man hangs for too long from the tree, and his weight will not do the job, his friends may seize his legs and pull him off. The high point of the dance is reached when all the Sun Dancers tear themselves free. All the women make the high, trembling, triumphant, brave, heart cry that reverberates from the hills. ▷

Sage is our most sacred herb. You burn it as incense. You rub yourself with it after a sweat. During a *yuwipi* ceremony you wear a sprig of sage in your hair or behind your ear. It makes the spirit come and speak to you. At the Sun Dance, the dancers wear wreaths of sage on their head and around the wrist. It's that sacred.

Myron Thompson, Sun Dancer, 1971

Sun Dancer, with sage wreath.

*Pine Ridge sun dancers blowing
on eaglebone whistles, 1972.*

This summer I pierced for the first time. As a young boy, I saw them
sun-dancing. It was so beautiful. I didn't understand it until later on.
There was a real strong feeling between people, between different
tribes. It was so good. I seen the men with their long hair flowing, the
women in their buckskin dresses. It was so beautiful it made me weep.
I wanted to be part of this. I wanted to feel this, spiritually and in my
flesh. Because I had been raised as a Christian, it was new to me. It was
so real compared to what I had known. So I made the commitment to
dance. I danced to get my older brother out of prison.

Bobby Leader Charge, aged 16, 1977

Merle Left Hand Bull blowing on plumed whistle.

I blew on my eaglebone whistle in rhythm to my dancing. The sound drowned out my pain. It made me see things with my mind. I saw an eagle circling over me. At first I thought it was a dream, but then I opened my eyes and saw it was real. The eagle had heard my whistle. I became part of that eagle.

Merle Left Hand Bull, 1971
at Rosebud Grass Mountain Sun Dance

Tipis at sunset.

DEFENDING THE DREAM

(civil rights)

Men were meant to live in tipis, not in boxes you call apartments. You have changed men into time-clock punchers and women into housewives—truly fearful creatures.

You live in prisons you have built for yourselves, calling them "homes, offices, factories." You know what that culture deprivation is that the anthros always talk about? It's being a white middle-class kid living in a split level apartment with color TV. I'd exchange such a no-good apartment any time for one of our beautiful old Lakota tipis.

Lame Deer

I Want The White Man Beside Me, Not Above Me

With these few words, Sitting Bull expressed the feelings of millions of Indians through the ages. The struggle for Indian rights began when the first white man set foot on this Turtle Continent. For centuries, the voice of the Native American went unheard. Indians did not write, they spoke no English. At first, a few knowledgeable and sympathetic whites spoke for them, men like John Colliers and James Mooney, or women like Helen Hunt Jackson who, through her book, *A Century of Dishonor*, tried to awaken the conscience of white America. Beginning in the nineteenth century, at the same time that whites were speaking in the name of "their Indians," a small group of native, tribal people—a mere trickle at the outset—made themselves heard. These were men and women who needed no interpreters. They came from the White Man's schools, out of Carlisle and Hampton, which were supposed to turn out farmers or domestics. Here they were in tweeds and velvet skirts, poised and eloquent.

There was Carlos Montezuma, M.D., "The Fierce Apache," snatched up as an infant from a pile of 30 lifeless bodies of his people, victims of a brutal massacre. Sold as a slave to a Mexican family for twenty dollars, he was redeemed and adopted by a reporter of the Chicago *Sun*. Educated at Brooklyn and Urbana, Illinois, and a physician in the Indian Service, he was a marvelous drawing card as a lecturer. (But would you want him to deliver *your* baby?) Montezuma used strong words, similar to the sayings of today's activist Indians, calling the reservations "houses of destruction" and "America's Siberias." He called the Bureau of Indian Affairs the "Indians' Bastille which had to be destroyed so that Native Americans could advance over its ruins to a better life." Strangely prophetic words.

There was Ohiyesa, better known as Dr. Charles Eastman, a Wahpeton Sioux whose father had been sentenced to hang for having taken part in the "Great Sioux Uprising" of Minnesota in the 1860s. (He was reprieved by President Lincoln, but served a long prison sentence.) Eastman went from missionary school to Dartmouth and Boston Medical School, and became a prolific writer of popular books about the American Indians' plight. Hailed as the "nation's best-known Indian," Eastman, a passionate believer in the redeeming force of Christianity, saw his beliefs destroyed when he viewed the shattered bodies of Sioux women and children after the massacre of Wounded Knee.

There was Arthur Parker, a Seneca, descendant of the prophet and religious reformer, Handsome Lake. Parker was a man of many hats—museum official, editor, writer, lecturer, archaeologist, anthropologist, activist. He was a so-called "progressive," a dapper, conservatively dressed man who condemned the wearing of native dress as "playing Indian." He felt that the solution to his people's problems was for them to join the White Man's society as equals in the melting pot. But if Parker walked the White Man's Road, he walked it as an Indian. "The true aim of educational effort," he said once, "should not be to make the Indian a white man, but simply a man *normal to his environment*."

One outstanding feature of this budding group of Native American activists was the important role that strong-minded women played in it. Among them were the La Flesche sisters, Susette and Susan, members of a prolific family from the Omaha tribe which, almost miraculously and instantaneously, produced anthropologists, doctors, teachers, artists, writers, poets, lecturers, librarians, and religious proponents. The first to make her impact felt was Susette, better known as Bright Eyes. Educated in Elizabeth, New Jersey, she returned to her people to become a teacher in a reservation school. When the peaceful Ponca tribe, known for its friendship to the whites, was brutally driven from its ancestral lands, Susette made herself the spokeswomen for the unfortunate exiles, traveling east to plead the Ponca cause. Her grace and dignity, as well as the emotional quality of her speech, made a tremendous impression upon white audiences. In the public mind she was instantly stereotyped as "The Indian Maiden," the "New Minnehaha," or "The Gentle Doe of the Prairie." She helped influence legislation which stopped the forcible removal of Indian tribes, and produced a Supreme Court decision which stated that "*An Indian is a Person*." Susette's younger sister, Susan, became a physician at a time when even white women doctors were seldom encountered. Both sisters devoted themselves to the Indian cause. Susan wrote: "La Flesche means Arrow—an arrow pointed at the enemies of our people."

Another fierce fighter for native rights was Laura Cornelius, an Oneida from Wisconsin, who refused to "genuflect before the altar of white progress." She condemned big cities, together with the whole economic, technical, office, and factory complex, proposing instead industrial villages carefully blended with the environment within large areas of carefully protected wilderness. She did not oppose the prevailing system because it was white, "but because it is unnatural and in the end will not work."

These men and women, as well as numerous others, were white-educated elitists. They organized a "National Indian Day." They lectured in churches and Masonic temples, at Cooper Union, Harvard, and Yale. They preached against demon rum and in favor of temperance. In 1911 they founded their own organization, the Society of American Indians. Their first membership conference was held on Columbus Day in Columbus, Ohio—"Indians discovering White America!" They came in serge and broadcloth, not a feather or breech-cloth among them. They overtipped. They were enthusiastically received by the public for "behaving so white." But one of their first acts was to deny white members the right to vote or to be part of the decision–making process. Whites could be "associate members at higher dues."

Young Indians today look down upon these forerunners in the fight for Indian rights as a bunch of "whitemanizing, Christianizing Hiawathas, Pocahontas, and Tontos," but they were the vanguard which laid the path. Also, they were above old inter-tribal quarrels and jealousies, the first true "pan-Indianists."

The two World Wars had a decisive effect upon the Indian civil rights movement. Native Americans had served with distinction in Europe and Asia. They had seen something of the world. There was Ira Hayes, the Pima Indian who had raised the Stars and Stripes over Mount Suribachi on Iwo Jima and won the Congressional Medal of Honor, but who died young, drunk, and pennyless. In 1944, the National Congress of American Indians (NCIA) was founded. Native Americans then had their own congress, with permanent headquarters in Washington, D.C., to represent the great family of tribes. It became an Indian lobby, "a red watchdog who barked loudly whenever anti-Indian legislation was in the making." NCIA was, and is, essentially conservative, a sort of Indian NAACP. Its directors are often tribal presidents. It is very effective, but does not excite "the young warriors and warrior women."

The Great Indian War of our time, many said, started with the founding of the National Indian Youth Council at Chicago in 1961. The participants probed, discussed, and commented upon the whole spectrum of Indian life. After due deliberation, they published a number of papers under the title, "What the Indian Wants." What they in fact produced was an Indian Bill of Rights. In its preamble is said:

> WE BELIEVE in the inherent right of all people to retain spiritual and cultural values, and that the free exercise of these values is necessary to the normal development of any people...

The declaration concluded:

> What we ask of America is not charity, not paternalism, even when benevolent. We ask only that the nature of our situation be recognized and made the basis of policy and action.

The founders of the National Indian Youth Council were college educated. Their motto was: "The young people must speak out." And speak they did—brilliantly. What they had to say shocked white listeners: "They didn't care for verbal fig leaves, they used words like war clubs." They were the intellectual spearhead of the Indian movement. Some called them "the New Indians." But as Laura Cornelius had already said:

"I am not the new Indian. I am the old Indian adjusted to new conditions." This was paraphrased by Dennis Banks into:

"They call us the new Indians. Hell, we are the old Indians, the landlords of this continent, coming to collect the rent."

Among these young leaders was Mel Thom, a Piute, who later became chairman of his Walker River Tribe, and Clyde Warrior, a Ponca Indian from Oklahoma, possibly the fiercest of this group, who died when still in his twenties. "He told it like it is," said a friend. "Clyde is dead, and in this year, 1968, Indians still die young."

Also among the legendary Indians of the sixties was Vine Deloria, a Standing Rock Sioux, who was the author of many books, an educator, and a lawyer, of whom it was said: "Vine was the great thinker of this period of Indian turmoil, one who gave to the whole movement his own distinct Indian philosophy."

Another member of this group was Hank Adams, an Assiniboin from Fort Peck, Montana, who later became a leader for Indian fishing rights on the Northwest Coast and founder of the Survival of the American Indian association.

Finally, among them should also be counted John Belindo, a Navajo-Kiowa, one of the youngest directors of NCIA, and Richard Oaks, a Mohawk from St. Regis, a leader during the occupation of Alcatraz who was murdered by a white man whom the law let go free.

The young New Indians who set the intellectual climate of the early sixties went the way of all flesh, but not before accomplishing their alloted task. Willowy girls became smiling mothers, and former firebrands became respected tribal leaders and educators. To the brash, slum-raised, uneducated young AIM warriors, who spoke with their bodies rather than their lips, the people from the National Indian Youth Congress could say, "We have built and launched the canoe, you paddle it!"

The war of words ended with the great "fish-ins" of Frank's Landing and other Washington State sites, "The first multitribal action of its kind since Hunkpapas, Minneconjous, Oglalas, and Cheyennes settled Custer's hash." The fight was against game and fishing laws which would put Indians, for whom fishing was a matter of survival, under the same restriction as white sportsmen who fished for amusement. This was no polite confrontation, but a series of arrests, jailings, clubbings, and handcuffing. During this Hank Adams was shot, but luckily survived.

AIM, the American Indian Movement, was born from the womb of the ghettoes and prisons of America. It was proud of its origins. Its founders were Clyde Bellecourt, Dennis Banks, Eddie Benton, and George Michell, all Ojibway (Chippewa) Indians from various Minnesota reservations. They defined themselves thus:

"AIM is the new warrior class of this century, bound by the bond of the drum, who vote with their bodies instead of their mouths. Their business is hope." AIM has been likened to the Black Panthers. It caused similar fear and consternation among the citizens of St. Paul and the ranchers of South Dakota. As one member said: "AIM was beautiful. It also had its warts and scars. Regardless, it was necessary. It made winos into warriors. It gave us pride and purpose."

Dennis Banks reminisced: "After organizing Minneapolis, we expanded and formed a chapter in Cleveland where we met a young forceful guy, an Oglala from Pine Ridge, who became our first board chairman in that city."

The young man was Russel Means—charismatic, eloquent, unpredictable, and battle-scarred—probably the best known of all the AIM leaders. He brought about the fusion of Ojibway and Sioux which put AIM on the map. The original members were all Ojibway city dwellers. Few of them spoke their language or knew much of their people's ancient culture or religion, which were in danger of dying out, although the medicine man, Eddie Benton, had taught some of them. Among the Sioux, the Ojibway found people who still performed the ancient rituals and spoke the Lakota language. Soon, men like Dennis Banks and Clyde Bellecourt were sun-dancing with the Sioux. Leonard Crow Dog became AIM's medicine man, ably assisted by Wallace Black Elk. Later, Philip Deere, a Muskogee Indian from Oklahoma, became the spiritual leader not only of AIM, but of concerned Indians in general. AIM soon made many converts among the Sioux and other tribes.

There were takeovers in a number of places. The occupation of Alcatraz in November, 1969 was a major event. It was not AIM-led or inspired, but among the occupants were a number of young people who later became prominent in the American Indian Movement. They called themselves "Indians of all Tribes." They held the "Rock" for more than one year. In the words of one of them, Ohoosis, a Cree from Canada:

"To all of us, November 20, 1969 was a fateful day, the day we took over Alcatraz Island. Alcatraz shouted out to the Indian people. Its lighthouse was a magnet for hundreds of young Indian men and women. Alcatraz was like a spark which started a big fire, many fires,

"Trail of Broken Treaties" takeover of Bureau of Indian Affairs Building, Washington D.C., November, 1972.

fires which the white mind could not even comprehend."

In 1971, Indians occupied the "Big Schlockstore Ashtray," Mount Rushmore. From the top of Teddy Roosevelt's head, the Sioux medicine man, Lame Deer, reclaimed the Sacred Black Hills for his people.

In November, 1972, the "Trail of Broken Treaties" ended in Washington, D.C. with the takeover of the Bureau of Indian Affairs Building—the Indians' Bastille. The Trail had been planned and organized by Robert Burnette, a Rosebud Sioux, twice tribal chairman and once director of NCIA. A moderate, Martin Luther King type of man, Burnette saw the event taken over by AIM. The occupation brought men like Dennis Banks, Russel Means, and Clyde Bellecourt to the notice of white Americans from coast to coast.

February 1973 brought the burning of the courthouse at Custer, South Dakota, a protest against the murder of an Indian, Wesley Bad Heart Bull, and the acquittal of his white killer. This was followed immediately by the occupation of Wounded Knee, the massacre site where hundreds of Sioux women and children had been killed by soldiers of Custer's old Seventh Cavalry. It was AIM's moment of glory. A small group of Indian boys and girls held off an army of marshals equipped with heavy machine guns, helicopters, and armed personnel carriers for 71 days. Two Indians were killed. A boy baby was born under fire to Mary Ellen, now married to Crow Dog.

Wounded Knee was followed by arrests and jailings. AIM faded from the national conscience and the television screens. Leaders were killed or they settled down.

The fight for Indian rights slumbers. It is not dead. It merely hibernates like seeds beneath the snow. ▷

Floyd Young Horse, painted for war, with homemade spear.

Dennis Banks, 1972.

Before the American Indian Movement, there were more suicides among Indians than among any other racial group in the United States. Young people drank themselves to death and sniffed glue. They lived in despair. They wore neckties and cut their hair short trying to look like white men. They were ashamed to be Indian. They were ashamed of their language and their Indian ways. At Wounded Knee they became warriors again and began feeling good about themselves, feeling good about being Sioux, and Cheyennes, Ojibway, Navajos, Crees, Iroquois, Saulteaux, and Nisquallys. They put on red face paint, let their hair grow, and proudly wore their ribbon shirts and angry hats. They called themselves "Skins" and stopped being whitemanized welfare recipients. Under fire they learned to respect themselves once more and, after almost one hundred years, they were ghost-dancing again. Even if AIM had not achieved anything else, it would have fulfilled its job.

Dennis Banks, 1973

Longest Walk tipi in front of White House, 1977.

We walked all the way from the Pacific to the Atlantic, from San Francisco to Washington. We put up our tepee here in front of the White House. Maybe the President in there will see us, or, maybe, he's watching football. But that doesn't concern us any more. We are marching.

Maynard Stanley
Passamaquoddy, 1977

PART TWO

Margo with Cigarstore Indian.

They stereotype us. First we are the red fiends, the red devils. Then we became the Boy Scouts' Indians—the "Noble Savages," the "Red Knights of the Prairie." Now they call us militants and non-acculturated aborigines. But we are not cigarstore Indians—definitely not.

Margo Thunderbird, Shinnecock, 1975

Roger Little Horn, Jr. and friend, drumming and singing at Wounded Knee Rally NYC before U.N., 1973.

RED ON

Now I can thank you, sir, for the polluted air
And for the hundreds of times that you cut my hair
'Cause after four hundreds of years of not seeming to care
It's about time I take the stand and about time I swear
I'm going to give my life to my brother the tree,
And for the mountain trout that flow free in the streams
And for the death of the fences that display lust and greed
And for the time that my Indian people can see
The day we can determine our own destiny
And for the day we can unite as a people and say. . .

red on?

David Red Bird, Ojibway

Portrait of Leonard Crow Dog.

A prison doctor asked me, "Have you ever been sick?" I told him, "No, I have never been sick, but I have this irritation." One of the doctors asked me, "Is it your eardrum that is irritated?" I said, "No, it is the government that is irritating and hurting me. The judges, I cannot digest their words; their words have no taste, no flavor. It has always been the government who broke their word. Do you have a cure for lying?" The white doctors didn't know how to take it.

I told my wife, "They have taken everything from me. They have taken Crow Dog's land, they have taken my elements, but, most important of all, they have taken my human body away from my people." I ask the Great Spirit: "Let me be the Earth, let me be the wind for my people."

Leonard Crow Dog, 1975

Portrait of Rod Skenandore.

I am not angry at any particular white man. You know, as they say, "some of my best friends are white." But I'm sure angry at the White Man's system he has imposed on us.

Rod Skenandore, Seneca

Lame Deer surrounded by rotting buffalo heads.

They have killed the buffalo, the holy food of the Indian, the buffalo, our brother, who gave his flesh so the people should live. But they're shooting them again, the so-called "surplus" buffalo at Custer State Park. They are the surplus buffalo and we are the surplus Indians. You can even buy a buffalo steak around here and buffalo burgers. The tourists love it, though it tastes like any other hamburger but costs twice as much. It's very sad.

Pete Catches, Oglala Sioux medicine man

Mary Ellen Crow Dog.

I had my baby at Wounded Knee in the middle of a fire fight. Two bullets went through the trailer in which I gave birth, but I was so busy being in labor I never noticed them.

I could hear the people outside. When they heard my little boy's first tiny cry all the women gave the high-pitched trembling Brave Heart Yell. I could see them through the window with their fists raised in the air. Then I felt that I had really accomplished something for my people.

Mary Ellen Crow Dog

Taos Pueblo, Taos, New Mexico.

PART THREE ▶▶▶

LIVING
THE DREAM

(people of the land)

The Earth is a living thing. The Mountains speak. The trees sing. Lakes can think. Pebbles have a soul. Rocks have power.

Lame Deer

Havasupai, Arizona.

Native Americans have a strong belief that they are responsible for the Earth's well-being. A Hopi elder said in an address to the government: "This land is the sacred home of the Hopi people and all the Indian race in this land. It was given to the Hopi people the task to guard this land, not by force of arms, not by killing, not by confiscation of properties of others, but by humble prayers, by obedience to our traditions and religious instructions, and by being faithful to our creator, Masau'u.

Thomas Benyacya, Hopi

Rosebud Sioux Reservation,
South Dakota.

The White Man did one good thing—he brought us Sunka-Wakan, the Holy Dog, namely the horse. It sure transformed our lives, made us the best light cavalry in the world, as Custer said, and he should know. When the skunk wagon breaks down, the horse still has enough gas.

Lame Deer

Yellowstone National Park.

The animals which the Great Spirit put here must go, says the Wasichu. The man-made animals are allowed to stay—at least until they are shipped out to be butchered. The terrible arrogance of the White Man, making himself something more than God, saying, "I will let this animal live, because it makes money"; saying, "This animal must go, it brings no income, the space it occupies can be used in a better way. The only good coyote is a dead coyote!" They are treating coyotes almost as badly as they used to treat Indians.

Lame Deer, 1969

Black Hills, South Dakota.

The Black Hills are the home of the Wakinyan, the Thunderbirds. They have no body, but have huge wings. They have no head, but they have beaks. They have no feet, but they have claws. They have no eyes, but they have lightning shoot out of those eyes which aren't there! The White Man built his gigantic ashtray, Mount Rushmore, right in the middle of Wakinyan land!

Lame Deer, 1971

Black Hills, South Dakota.

The Mako Sica, the Badlands, were the home of the great watermonster Unktegila and her children. Their giant bones were strewn all over the place. Once, when I was young, I was caught on a ridge in the Badlands in the middle of the night. Also in the middle of a terrific storm. I dared not walk on that ridge. I straddled it like a horse and slid along it. I didn't know what was at the right or left of me, how deep it might be. I sure was scared. Then when the light of a big flash of lightning lit up the darkness, I saw that I was riding on bones—Unktegila's spine!

Lame Deer, 1969, in Badlands

Bryce Canyon, Utah.

The Sun still shines on our beautiful mesas, but for how long?

Thomas Benyacya

Monument Valley, Utah.

PEOPLE OF
THE PLAINS

Ways of the People

Photographs of Plains people were taken on two Sioux Reservations in South Dakota: at the Lame Deer, Montana, reservation of the Northern Cheyenne, and at the Crow Agency, also in Montana. These tribes, though they speak different languages, share a common Plains culture. After acquisition of firearms and the horse (universally called the Holy Dog or Spirit Dog), the nations of the Great Prairies entered into a Golden Age, characterized by a free-roaming life which centered upon the buffalo that covered the Plains from horizon to horizon. Life was sweet, particularly for the men. Hunting and warfare became their glorious sports. As an Indian poster put it:

"Before the White Man came we had no lawyers, no jails, no banks, no taxes, and no TV. Women did all the work. White Man thought he could improve upon a system like that."

This Golden Age lasted only about 75 years. Then the wasichu conquered the land. Smallpox and whisky wiped out whole native tribes. The buffalo, upon which the Indians' material culture and food supply depended, were exterminated by white buffalo hunters and their teams of skinners. The tribes were driven into so-called reservations and fenced in. The former "Red Knights of the Prairie" were turned into wards of the government, forced to live on handouts, their religion and way of life suppressed.

Some reservations are big. Rosebud and Pine Ridge, for instance, together cover some three million acres, but most of the land is leased to white ranchers. The landscape is primarily rolling prairie, good for grazing, but poor farm country. Some 20,000 Sioux now live on the two contiguous reservations. There are spots of beauty—some lakes and pine-studded hills, a winding river, and spectacular badlands of fantastic erosions. To the north are the Paha Sapa, the Sacred Black Hills, home of the Thunderbirds and, in defiance of solemn treaties, stolen from the Sioux to be turned into a tourist playland.

There are many problems. Unemployment reaches 80 percent. There are few jobs and no meaningful employment, no industries. Poverty is staggering. This results in alcoholism—the sure sign of despair. There is tension between the minority of traditional full-bloods in the back country and the slightly better-off *iyeskas*, the half-bloods, who get most of the tribal jobs. But the people's spirit is unbreakable. The old language is still being spoken, the old rituals performed. There is a sharing spirit. Those who have a little, share with those who have nothing. The people are sociable, fond of pow-wows

70

and get-togethers, of joking and joshing, of visiting back and forth. Grownups, even friends, may savage each other in drunken brawls, but child abuse is unknown. Tribal folks who live in faraway cities are still connected by their "umbilical cords" to the reservations.▷

I love to tell stories to children, old stories handed down from generation to generation. Funny stories about Iktome, the smart-ass spiderman, scary stories about ghosts, sad stories about maidens dying of love, brave-heart stories about Sioux warriors counting coup in battle. Such tales keep our spirits and language alive.

Lame Deer, 1968

Lame Deer telling stories to children.

Mrs. Strange Owl in front of her cabin, hanging up jerk meat.

I live alone in this little log cabin. It's big enough. I'm making jerk meat, hanging it up to dry. Come back in a month when its ready. Then we have a feast.

Mrs. Strange Owl, Cheyenne, Birney, Montana

Maggie and great granddaughter on Rosebud Reservation (White River settlement).

I'm Maggie Six Shooter. This is my little great granddaughter. They tell me I'm going blind. I don't mind. If you're blind you can see things so much better—in your mind, in your heart.

Maggie Six Shooter, White River, S.D., 1976

Henry talking and gesticulating in his shack. Rosebud, 1972.

The planes won't fly, the rockets won't go up. The bomb won't work. Somebody will turn off the electricity. The computers go crazy. The whole goddamn system, the wasichu system will break down. The commanders and generals, the senators and the millionaires, the president himself and all the scientists, won't know what to do. They'll wind up eating snakes, nothing but snakes!

Henry Crow Dog, 1981

Henry playing flute.

Hehaka, the elk, loves to hang around with womenfolk. He has a good voice. He's a musician. The elk master, the fellow with the elk medicine, he has a flute. The girl hears it and comes running. She can't resist.

The elk is formed like a tree with branches. We use his antlers to bring the glowing rocks into the sweat lodge.

Hehaka spirit is a flute spirit. The *siyotanka*, the flute, plays so nice even the animals in the wood love it. *Hehaka siyotanka*—the elk flute. That's for making love. You play the flute, the next morning the deer are around and a good spirit comes.

The elk is gentle. He puts himself between his herd and the wind, between his women and danger, to protect them.

The women hear the flute, they scratch themselves, hitch up their skirts. They feel it. Nobody has to tell them, *wi-shan pastanka*.

Hehaka lowanpi, the elk ceremony. Then you could sing the *hehaka olo-wan*. The *hehaka*, he has the love wink in his eye.

The deer, the elk man. The cedar smell gives this man the power to dream.

Henry Crow Dog, 1969

75

Floyd Young Horse picking herbs.

We have all kinds of herbs we use for healing and for our ceremonies. Some herbs you got to pray to before you pick them, some of them you should only approach from upwind or downwind. There are so many herbs we use—for a cough, for wounds, for broken bones, or for a stopped-up water bag [bladder]. We even have herbs for a woman to have or not to have a baby. These you use with great caution. But the big chief of all herbs is the Sacred Sage.

Lame Deer, 1970

Large coup stick planted next to grave-stone of Seventh Cavalry Trooper, Custer Battlefield.

My grandfather, Wooden Legs, was still a teenager when he fought against Custer, way back in 1876. He took a funny scalp—one of the mutton chops, they also call them dundrearies, off Captain Cook. I still have it hanging somewhere. It looks like a ratty fox tail. That crooked stick is an old coup stick. You touched an enemy with it while he was still alive and armed. That was a coup, a war honor. That earned him an eagle feather. It does my heart good to see that old coup stick planted on the battle field where we and the Sioux won the great victory.

John Wooden Legs, Tribal Chairman
Northern Cheyennes, Lame Deer, Montana, 1966

Henry Crow Dog.

I'm a full-blood. There are not many left. I'm the real thing and proud of it. My grandfather fought Custer. He killed Chief Spotted Tail in a fight and almost got hanged for it. He was the first Mister Indian to win a case in the Supreme Court. He was a Ghost Dancer Leader. He got four wounds in battle—two bullets and two arrows. He could speak with coyotes. He's in the history books. I'm flesh from his flesh.

Henry Crow Dog, 1971

Lame Deer in New York on top of Rockefeller Center in full regalia.

Look at that smog! Look at all those little ants running around down there! They're people! The Statue of Liberty! They are always talking about it. But she faces the wrong way. She turns her back on Mister Indian. She tells the white men from across the ocean, "Come on! Steal some more Indian Land!"

Lame Deer

Portrait of Archie.

When my father lay dying he called for me. He laid his hands upon my head, gave me his Sacred Pipe, and passed on to me his power to carry on as a medicine man.

Archie Fire Lame Deer

Mrs. He Dog, Parmelee, Rosebud Reservation.

I was born long before they had a census. So I never got a Christian name. I'm just Mrs. He Dog. I don't even know how old I am. Over 100, at any rate. You should have taken my picture 80 years ago when I was still pretty. Yes, I was very pretty. A lot of fine young men were courting me. Now I have a face as if somebody had deep-plowed it. That's okay. Old age has been good to me.

Mrs. He Dog, Parmalee, Rosebud Reservation

Girl rider with elktooth dress.

That girl over there has a hundred-elk-tooth outfit. Only the eyeteeth are used. That's something to see.

Comment of a Crow Indian, 1967

Rachel Strange Owl in Dentalium Shell dress and baby. Lame Deer, Montana, Northern Cheyenne Reservation, 1972.

A nation is not conquered
Until the hearts of its women are on the ground.
Then it is finished,
No matter how brave its warriors
Or how strong their weapons.

Cheyenne proverb

Judy Bridwell.

Winyan kin akoka	You women,
Econpiye yo!	Keep away from me
Cicinpi sni yelo	I don't want you!
Sicangu winyan ecena wacin	I want
Ye!	a Rosebud Woman!
Sicangu Winyan,	Woman from Rosebud,
Washte cilake!	I love you!

Old Lakota love song

Three little Sioux girls playing.

Children are our greatest treasure. The new generation coming up. We won't disappear. We shall live!

Pete Catches, Oglala, Pine Ridge Reservation

PEOPLE OF THE MESAS

The Peaceful Ones

The Spanish word *pueblo* can mean either a people or a town. It is used as an overall term for the corn-planting, sedentary, and peaceful Indians of Arizona and New Mexico who belong to a number of language groups but share a common culture and lifestyle. The Pueblo Indians have traditions and customs that are markedly different from the Plains Indians. The Sioux and other prairie dwellers were nomadic hunters who followed the herds of buffalo. The Pueblos have been farmers since prehistoric times, planters of corn, squash, and beans. The Plains tribes never stayed long in one place. The Pueblos lived in permanent settlements generation after generation. The Plains Indians were warlike, fond of raiding and "counting coup" upon their enemies in ritual battle. The Pueblos were averse to violence, though capable of defending themselves with skill and courage—if they had to. The prairie folk were male-oriented. One of their favorite sayings was: "Woman shall not walk before man." The Pueblos live in a matriarchal society in which women have extraordinary powers. The Sioux pray to the spirit of the Buffalo, the Pueblos to the Corn Maidens.

The Pueblos are descendants of the early Basketmakers, of the "Old Ones," the Anasazi, the cave dwellers who built Cliff Palace at Mesa Verde, and Montezuma's Castle and Betatakin. Later ancestors built cities of stone such as Pueblo Bonito in Chaco Canyon, or Aztec Ruin. Years of drought, during which no rain fell, forced them to move south to the Rio Grande, some of them stopping for a while on the Pajarito Plateau and in Frijoles Canyon, where they scooped their dwelling from cliffs of soft volcanic tufa rock.

Long before the coming of the Spaniards, these Indian farmers were skilled in the arts of basket-making, weaving, pottery, feather blanket-making and the working of shell and turquoise into beautiful jewelry.

They hunted deer with the help of atlatls—spear-throwing sticks—or with bows and arrows. They went after small game with boomerang-shaped rabbit sticks. Work was divided between the sexes in accordance with a strangely Freudian symbolism. Men did the planting with a digging stick, and wove blankets or garments using the back-and-forth flitting shuttle. They wielded spears at the hunt or in war. They brought in the heavy roof beams, but women did much of the actual house building. Women also made baskets and pots, harvested the corn, and performed all tasks suggestive of conception, pregnancy, and birth-giving.

The Pueblo land is beautiful, sometimes wild and sometimes gentle, always varied. It is a vista of haunting deserts, enchanted mesas, badlands of contorted, multicolored erosions alternating with dark, moist forests and towering snow-capped mountain ranges. The country abounds with natural wonders such as painted deserts, petrified forests, and a gigantic meteor crater. Here also is the Grand Canyon, Monument Valley, Canyon de Chelly, and the four holy mountains that are sacred to Pueblos and Navajos alike.

The history of the Pueblo Indians stretches far back in time, much farther back than that of the Plains Indians. It is a history that is thrilling, capricious, and often tragic. The first outsiders to arrive in Pueblo land were a Franciscan friar, Marcos de Niza; Estevanico, his black slave; and a number of Mexican-Indian porters. They traveled through inhospitable desert country, lured by rumors of the fabled, exceedingly rich, Seven Cities of Cibola, where streets were paved with gold, and children played with baubles of emeralds, rubies, and diamonds. And so, these first humans from across the ocean were "a blackamoor, whose amorous propensities lured him to his death," and a priest, of whom one early writer said that "his reports were so disgustful of lyes and wrapped up in fictions that the light was little more than darkness."

To be specific, Estevanico, ranging ahead of his master, reached the Zuni village of Hawikuh, where he made sexual advances to the women, whose outraged husbands threw him down "from a high place." The good friar never dared to do more than view Hawikuh from afar, plant a cross, and take formal possession of all the land in the name of the Spanish king, after which he fled back to Mexico as fast as his sandaled feet would carry him. Having seen the evening sun reflected from Hawikuh's walls and houses, he reported to the viceroy that he had found Cibola and that, indeed, it was built of gold and silver.

In 1540, on the strength of the friar's report, Don Francisco de Coronado, a gentleman-adventurer, led a force of 75 horsemen and numerous foot soldiers and porters to possess himself of the fabled Seven Cities' treasures. The Spaniards' motto, then and later, as expressed by one caballero, was: "We come here for the love of God, the glory of the king, and also to get rich," or, as Hernando Cortez remarked, "I came here for gold, not to toil like a peasant."

Coronado stormed Hawikuh against desperate resistance, killing many of its inhabitants. He found neither gold, nor precious stones, but robbed the villagers of their food supply and woven blankets. His men destroyed a number of pueblos, suppressed uprisings, and got as far as Kansas in their futile search for gold. In 1542, they gave up and returned to Mexico. Coronado reported that he had counted 71 Indian villages, considerably more than there are today. For almost 50 years, the Pueblos were left in peace, but in 1598, Don Juan de Onate arrived with many Spaniards, not to search for gold but to settle. The Spaniards conquered the Pueblos with the help of a number of "wonder weapons": horses, armor, swords of steel, and "firesticks," or cannon and matchlocks. The soldiers and settlers were followed by missionary priests. Soon every village had to admit two or three of them. In most pueblos, massive churches were erected by Indian forced labor.

Friars appropriated Indian land for their own use, forced native women to become their mistresses, and looked upon the Indian as their slaves. In one pueblo the friars had an Indian cruelly beaten for having prayed to his ancient gods. They then smeared him with pitch and set him aflame. The Spanish settlers and officials did not treat the natives any better. A common saying was that "between the upper grindstone of the caballeros and the nether grindstone of the friars, the indio is ground into dust."

Indian religion was cruelly suppressed. The friars complained that "[the Indians] dance publicly introducing many superstitious and scandalous acts in these dances, using subterranean places that they call estufas [kivas] in which they invoke the devil and commit a thousand grievous errors." So the Pueblos' ceremonies were outlawed, the kivas destroyed, and the sacred masks burned. In 1675, 47 "sorcerers and witches," that is, medicine men and native priests, were tried as heretics. Three were publicly hanged, the rest flogged until their flesh hung in shreds and then jailed. Among the victims was Popé, a medicine man from San Juan, described as "a man who should either be treated gently, or killed." Popé eventually fled to Taos, where he organized the Great Pueblo Revolt of 1680.

All of the Pueblos, from the Hopi villages in Arizona to the village of Taos, rose as one, killing their missionaries and tearing down the churches. Many Spaniards lost their lives. The survivors cut their way through an army of enraged Indians, taking refuge in El Paso. Not a single white man was left in Pueblo land.

In 1692, led by Don Diego de Vargas, the Spaniards came back in force to reconquer their lost province. The Indians were brutally punished and a number of villages destroyed. The Church had, however, learned its lesson. Suppression of native religion had led to the Great Revolt and was thus realized to be impossible. A compromise was reached: the Indians would become outwardly Christian while, at the same time, continuing to practice their ancient beliefs. As Matilda Stevenson summed it up:

"The Pueblos are in fact as non-Catholic as before the Spanish conquest, holding their ceremonies in secret, practicing their occult powers to the present time, under the very eyes of the Church. The Catholic priest marries the betrothed, but they have previously been united according to their ancestral rites. The Romish priests hold Mass that the dead may enter heaven, but prayers have already been offered that the soul may be received by Sus-sis-tin-na-ko, their Creator, into another world. Though professedly Catholic, they await only the departure of the priest to return to their ancient ceremonials." (Stevenson)

In 1821, when Mexico gained its independence, the Southwest fell under Mexican administration. In 1846 it became part of the United States. Since then, the three races—Anglo, Hispanic, and Indian—have lived peacefully side by side. The pueblos are tiny, self-governing city states. In the words of an early observer, Charles Lummis: "The Pueblo Indians have a complete government of their own, each village being an independent and full-fledged republic, with a great body of sound and sensible laws, and with perfectly competent machinery to enforce them and to administer justice." (Lummis, p. 401)

At the head of the traditional pueblo government stands the *cacique*, or chief. The Hopis call such a man *kikmongwi*, the Zuni, *pekwin*, the Keresan-speaking villages, *traikatse* or *tiamuny*. Essentially the cacique is a priest.

The Americans introduced a parallel, Washington-style, tribal government that is headed by a governor and supported by a tribal council. In some places, most recently among the Hopis, the two types of government, traditional and white-style, are at loggerheads. In other villages they work harmoniously together.

Every village is made up of a number of clans, usually named after animals or plants. A pueblo also contains a number of kivas, which are sacred ceremonial chambers that are sometimes square but often round, located underground or partially above ground. In the kivas, religious societies meet and young men are instructed in the beliefs and ceremonies of their people. Kivas are also used for non-religious gatherings. The prehistoric Anasazi towns all had kivas, sometimes as many as a dozen.

The status of women among the Pueblos is extraordinarily high. Descent is traced through the mother. The houses and garden patches are owned by the women. Husbands move into their wives' homes. Children are spoken of as "belonging to the mother."

Houses are sometimes made of stone, but more often of adobe. D.H. Lawrence wrote: "That they don't crumble is a mystery. That these little squarish mud heaps endure for centuries after centuries, while Greek marble tumbles asunder, and cathedrals totter, is a wonder. But then, the naked human hand with a bit of new, soft mud is quicker than time, and defies history."

The Pueblos are deeply religious. Their daily life is inseparably intermingled with their spiritual life. One writer remarked that, if religion were removed from the warp and woof of Pueblo existence, there would be preciously little left. These people believe in the omnipresence of a number of worlds that are stacked up, one upon the other. When humans become evil and no longer take good care of the Earth, their particular world is destroyed. A few survivors then climb a cornstalk or pine trunk through an opening in the sky vault into a new world. This opening is called the *sipapu*—the hole of emergence. Traditional Hopis of today are warning us that our modern world is threatened with impending destruction, destined to be replaced by a new one, unless we mend our exploitive and ecologically disastrous ways.

Pueblos are wedded to their land, tending the same fields generation after generation. Thomas Benyacya said, "We were told by Masauw, the Creator: 'This is your land. Keep it for me until I come back.' " The Pueblo Indians have always been here as hunters and gatherers, as basket makers, as cliff dwellers, and as contemporary American citizens. The Southwest is their land, on which they have dwelled and planted their corn since the dawn of time. No wonder that they look with a little irony, and even pity, upon the newly arrived, footloose, and self-conscious Anglo. The Pueblos are, in this respect, much luckier than people from the former buffalo-hunting tribes who were driven from their ancient hunting grounds. The Pueblos are dry farmers par excellence, easily surmounting problems which would stagger white farmers. A Hopi can raise corn from desert sand.

Pueblo art is renowned for its beauty, and eagerly sought by collectors. Typical Pueblo crafts include pottery, basketry, jewelry, weaving, and the carving of so-called Kachina dolls. The last 25 years have also seen the emergence of internationally known Pueblo painters and sculptors. Each Pueblo has its own pottery designs that often originated in prehistoric times. It is no accident that Pueblo art is derived from Pueblo religion, and that among its chief motifs are many sacred symbols: corn and squash blossoms, corn maidens, Rainbowman, Thunderbird, and Sunfather.

Religious ceremonies are at the center of Pueblo existence. They play an essential role in keeping alive an age-old system, in maintaining the Pueblos self-identification, and in preserving a culture which had its birth more than a thousand years ago. These ceremonies symbolize a worldview. They represent a continuous mythical drama which stages itself, act by act, scene by scene, conforming to the course of the Sun and the flow of the seasons. These spiritual dramas are most often expressed as dances—prayers in motion.

Cemetery Guardian, Acoma.

There are many ritual dances. Some are supplications to the life-giving rain and corn spirits. Others are hunting dances to propitiate the spirits of animals who have given themselves as food for the people, and to make the animals willing to do so for eternity. These include the Buffalo, Deer, and Mountain Sheep Dances. There are also Eagle and Butterfly Dances; Rainbow, Cloud, Bow, and Basket Dances, and the famous Hopi Snake Dance, which is a prayer for rain. Of unsurpassed beauty are the masked Kachina Dances.

The nature of the *kachinas* can be best understood by an explanation given to me by a friend from Acoma: "Way back, in times we no longer remember, when our people were still living at White House, long before we settled in our Sky City of Acoma, the *katsina* used to visit us in person to dance for us. But then something happened, something bad, maybe, which made the *katsina* visit us no longer. But they allowed us to personify them by putting on their masks and performing their dances. If we do this, they told the people, they would always be present in spirit."

Thus the *kachinas* were benevolent supernaturals who, for instance, could make rain, and who, long ago, are supposed to have come in the flesh to the Hopi, Zuni, Acoma, and other Pueblos. A by-product of the *kachina* "mystery plays" are the well-known *kachina* dolls. Originally, these were given to children by the masked dancers to illustrate the different *kachinas*. As the children familiarized themselves with the dolls, they were told the legends of their pueblo and were taught the powers and characteristics of the various *kachinas*. Today, *kachina* dolls are frequently made for the tourist trade, often by non-Pueblo Indians or even whites. As a result, they are becoming gaudier and less authentic.

Among the Pueblo dancers, the sacred clowns or "delight makers," hold a special place. Called, depending on the tribe, *koyem-shi, kosa, chiffonetti*, or "mudheads" by some whites, they play a major part in many dances. John Collier, writing about the Zuni *koyemshi*, observed:

"Those clowns at the Shalako, those 'mudheads,' potent healers and cosmic comedians, who, almost naked, move through the slow hours in zero temperature with never a shudder of cold; their medicinal power is great, their traditional wisdom is believed even greater, and their organization is very ancient; the Zunis place their origin at the beginning of things." This sums up the nature of the Pueblo "clown," as well as that of the Sioux *heyoka*, the Cheyenne *veeho*, and all the other "tricksters" in the Indian universe.

The Pueblo people live their lives with a sense of natural perpetuity which, sadly, has disappeared from white American society.

It is a way of keeping the past fresh while absorbing the present, and hopefully the future, into an endlessly flowing stream of Pueblo spirit and personality. ▷

Birds-eye view of Pueblo Bonito.

They called us backwards and uncivilized, but our ancestors built the first apartment house complex in the whole world, here, almost 900 years ago.

Indian onlooker watching author
photographing Pueblo Bonito

Pictograph of horned masked head. Zuni, 1964.

You can see the images of our *kachinas* depicted on rock walls all over this country. Images of gods and men, of horned dancers and plumed serpents. They were made by our people hundreds of years ago.

Encarnacion Peña

Painted Desert, Arizona, 1985.

Before writing, as we know it, was discovered, there was "picture writing"—the so-called pictographs and petroglyphs. Pictographs are rock paintings. Petroglyphs are designs scratched or incised into boulders or the faces of cliffs. You can find them all over the world—inside the prehistoric caves of France and Spain, on large runic or Ogham stones in Scandinavia and Ireland, in the Sahara and the land of the Bushman. In America they can be found in Pennsylvania and on the Great Plains, in California and Utah. But, above all, it is the American Southwest, New Mexico and Arizona, where they are most abundant and where whole canyon walls are covered with them. There are images of humans and animals, of birds and snakes and masked shamans, of Sun and stars. Some of this rock art is of a magic, religious nature, other designs show the way to water, or out of a canyon, or where game is plentiful. Some trace the path of stars or the moment of an eclipse.

Richard Erdoes

Famous Navajo pictograph showing arrival of priest on horseback.

They came with the Bible in one hand and the gun in the other. First they stole gold. Then they stole the land. Then they stole souls.

Ginger Hillis, Navajo

Ghan (Mountain Spirit) dancer.

In the center of the Sacred Mountain,
At the place called "Home in the Turning Rock"
The Mountain Spirits, sacred, sacred,
Sing over me.
In the Center of the Sacred Mountain,
Stands a brush shelter,
Home of the Black Mountain Spirit.
With lightning flashing from my moccasins,
With lightning striking along my path,
My headdress lives.
Its jingles tinkling,
Its sound is heard!
My song embraces these dancers.

Mountain Spirit song, Apache

Ency in blanket and before fireplace.

I paint pictures of our pueblo's dances. I build adobe walls. They took me to Nepal to show me off as the old token Indian. In Nepal I wept. I really wept, because the people were so poor and the little children so hungry.

Encarnacion Peña

Sacred Clown dancing with corn dancers and Kisis hut in background.

All the Pueblos have their clown societies—*kosa* among the Tewa; *koyemshi* at Zuni; *chiffonetti* in Taos; and *koshare* at Acoma. Some have called them "delight-makers." But they are not like the white man's circus clown. They are sacred clowns; they perform a sacred dance. Even when people laugh at their antics, they are doing something sacred. Some have the power to make rain and others can make humans and animals get babies. For that reason the clowns can make very sexy jokes without anybody getting mad, except, maybe, some missionary.

Encarnacion Peña, San Ildefonso

Two cloud ladies.

There are always two cloud ladies beside the many male dancers. They volunteer to participate. They are always close relatives of the incoming officials—the wife, or the daughter, sometimes even the mother of a young official. So, besides being a rite of peace and harmony, the Cloud Dance also is held to ensure a good year for the new governor and his aides. The feathers on the two women dancers' heads represent clouds—cloud blossoms.

Professor Alfonso Ortiz, San Juan

Boy dancer, about seven or eight years old.

We introduce our children early to our ceremonies and let them participate in our dances. Some of the dancers are quite young. Some are mere toddlers. At the head of the dance line are the tallest grown-ups. After them in the line-up come the teenagers, then the young boys, then the little ones, so the dancers in line get smaller and smaller, with the youngest and littlest at the end.

Alfonso Ortiz, San Juan, Tewa

Eagle Dance at Zuni, 1964.

The eagle is the grandest of all birds. He has the greatest power. He communicates with the Ones Above. He can cure people's illnesses. His world is the air which is also the breath of life. In some places, such as the Hopi villages, they keep eagles on their roof tops. They need their feathers for prayer sticks and other sacred things, I'm told.

Comment of Navajo onlooker
at Gallup ceremonial

Taos man in turban and braids.

Ours is the northernmost pueblo. We were a meeting place where the white mountain men, the Spaniards, the Pueblos, and the Plains Indians met to trade. That's why we adopted some Plains traditions, like our men keeping their hair in braids like Comanches, or Kiowas, or Sioux.

Rosarita Romero, Taos, 1975

Santana baking bread in horno.

We still bake our bread in the beehive-shaped ovens the Hispanics call "hornos." You make a wood fire in the horno and then, when the inside is really hot, you rake the ashes out and put the bread in. It tastes better than the one you get at the supermarket. My husband is a baker. I should know.

Irma Maldonado-Antonio
Acoma, 1977

Santana, balancing olla on head.

When I was young, I went to the waterhole almost every day. It was hard balancing the heavy water olla on your head, leaving my hands free to grab the handholds dug into the rock with stone tools so many hundreds of years ago. Yes, it was a hard life when I was a young girl, but I wish myself back in those old days when everything was so unspoiled and beautiful. As you see, I can still balance my olla on my head.

Santana Antonio, 1977

Ancient Acoma stairs.

Those steps on the Padre's Trail which lead up to our ancient village of Acoma have been worn down by a thousand years of walking on them with our soft moccasins or bare feet.

Santana Antonio
Acoma, New Mexico, 1955

A World of Bright Radiance

The Spaniards named them Navajos, but they call themselves Dineh—the People. They live in a hard land of supernatural beauty to which they cling with a fierce, stubborn love. Mystery shrouds their origins. They belong to the family of Athabascan tribes, speaking a language closely related to that of the Deneh of the North who live in Canada and Alaska, more than a thousand miles distant from them.

To the People, the land in which they live is sacred. It was created by the Holy Ones for the Dineh to populate. Men and animals had to pass through four previous worlds before emerging into this one, the Fifth World of Bright Radiance. The Holy People put four sacred mountains at the corners of Navajo Country: to the East, the Mountain of White Shell (Mt. Blanca, Colorado); to the South, the Mountain of Blue Turquoise (Mount Taylor, New Mexico); to the West, the Mountain of Yellow Abalone (San Francisco Peak, Arizona); and to the North, the Mountain of Black Jet (Mount Hesperus, Colorado). The Holy Ones taught the People to live happily in this land, in harmony with the Earth, the streams, the plants, and the animals. The People responded:

> I see the Earth.
> I am looking at Her and smile
> Because She makes me happy.
> The Earth, looking back at me
> Is smiling too.
> May I walk happily
> And lightly
> Upon Her.

Some archaeologists place the arrival of the Navajos in the Southwest as early as 1000 A.D. By 1400 A.D. they had established themselves solidly in their new country. There seems to have been one great burst of immigration, followed by a succession of smaller immigrations extending over generations. They arrived by stages, staying for a while in one place and then wandering on. According to their own mythology, a legendary pair of the People started walking toward the West to Hole in the Ground. They kept on arriving at Swallow's Nest, then went to House-Under-The-Spreading-Out-Rock. Then they continued to Mistletoe Hangs and from there to Dead Tree Standing Up. Then they went to Possessing Fish. From there to Red House, then to Weed-Covered Lake.

The Dineh were a hardy and resourceful breed. They also had a knack for learning quickly, taking from other cultures what was useful. Upon their arrival, they were primitive nomads, the men hunting while the women and children gathered edible roots, nuts, seeds, and berries. In the summer, the men wore not much more than a G-string, the women a sort of apron made from shredded cedar bark. All wore rawhide moccasins—a must in a country of chapparal, thorn bushes, and cacti. In winter, both sexes wrapped themselves in animal hides and furs. They had weapons and tools made of stone, wood, and bone. Whatever they needed they fashioned with their own hands. Being warlike, they raided the granaries of the peaceful sedentary Pueblos. They also carried off Pueblo women who, while becoming wives and mothers, taught the Dineh the arts of weaving and pottery making. More importantly, they showed them how to plant corn. It appears that the Navajos had only to be exposed to something new and they would promptly adopt it for their own use.

After the coming of the Spaniards, they just as quickly realized the value of owning sheep and horses. As Wharton James put it: "After the Spaniards introduced sheep, it was not long before the Navajos were extensive sheep raisers. It would not be any wiser to enter into an inquiry as to the methods by which these flocks were acquired than it would be to ascertain the history of many of the landed possessions of European nobility." (Wharton James, p.130) It also took little time before the Navajo women began to weave sheep's wool into striped blankets and ponchos, the forerunners of the famous Navajo rugs of today.

Navajo history is marked with tragedy. The Spaniards invaded Navajo country, kidnapped Dineh women, and carried off children as future slaves. The Navajo, in turn, raided Spanish settlements and ranches to add to their stock of horses and sheep. The result was a perpetual state of war that lasted over 200 years. It was a war of muskets and cannon against bows and arrows, of iron-tipped lances and swords of steel against weapons made of stone and wood. The results were never in doubt.

On one of their punitive expeditions, the Spaniards trapped a band of Navajos in Canyon del Muerte—the Canyon of Death. The Indians sought refuge inside a large cave halfway up the canyon cliff. The Spaniards shot their muskets up into the cave, spraying it with bullets which ricocheted from the cave's roof and walls, killing the people inside one by one, including the women and children, until no one was left alive. The site has been known ever since as Massacre Cave.

After 1846, the whole Southwest came under the rule of the United States, of the *Norte Americanos*, but things did not change much. The Anglos committed atrocities against the Indians, and the Navajos raided the Americans' homesteads as they had raided the Spaniards and Mexicans before. In the frontier country, raiding was a way of life, almost a sport. In the view of the settlers, the only good Indian was a dead one. Territorial governors offered a bounty of ten dollars for every coyote, Apache, or Navajo scalp brought in. That kind of money attracted a breed of roughnecks known as bounty or scalp hunters—characters who, for ten dollars, would have killed their own grandmother. Life was cheap and scalp-hunting became a profitable business—so profitable that professional scalpers indiscriminately murdered Indians, Mexicans, and even white folks with black hair for the five or ten dollars of bounty money.

In 1862, the famous Indian Scout, Kit Carson, was sent to, once and for all, "settle the Navajo problem." He called the Dineh leaders together and gave them a choice: either surrender, or fight and be wiped out. The Navajos were determined to fight for their land and way of life. Carson declined to fight them on their own terms. Instead of following them into the canyons, where he would have been at a disadvantage, he laid waste to their land, destroying their crops, cutting down their fruit trees, and driving off their herds of livestock. Faced with starvation, the Navajos were forced to surrender. Carson rounded them up, and drove them to his headquarters at Fort Defiance. From there he marched his prisoners—7000 men, women and children—to a blistering hell-hole called Bosque Redondo, 300 miles away. It was a death march. There were no wagons for the infirm and the sick. The old and the ill dropped by the wayside to die. This Trail of Tears is still remembered with bitterness as the "Long Walk." Some call it the Navajos' Bataan.

When the survivors reached Bosque Redondo, they found that no arrangements had been made to receive them. There were not even tents. They were forced to dig holes in the ground like prairie dogs for shelter. The poor soil and a brutal climate made even bare subsistence impossible. In July, 1867, a Navajo spokesman told a government official:

"I am thinking all the time of my old country, hoping that the government will put us back there. We have worked here in heat and cold, and to no avail. What more can we do? What does the government want to do with us?"

In May, 1868, General William Sherman visited Bosque Redondo. He tried to persuade the Navajos to settle in the Indian territory of Oklahoma, but they stubbornly refused to go there. Speaking for the whole tribe, the headman, Barboncito, asked that his people be allowed to return to their "beloved red rock country":

"Our grandfathers had no thought of living in any other country than our own and it is not right we should abandon it. Here we plant, but the soil does not yield. Our animals have died. We have nothing left in the way of possessions but a gunnysack to wear during the day and to cover us at night. It makes my mouth dry and my head hangs low seeing us die here."

At last the government relented and allowed the Navajos to return to their ancestral home. It took them five weeks to get there, but this time they did not mind the hardships of the trail. Again, Barboncito spoke for all the people when he movingly said:

"After we get back to our country, it will brighten up again, and the Navajo will be as happy as the land. Black clouds will lift and there will be plenty of rain to make the corn grow. It will grow in abundance and we shall be happy."

The Navajos live on the largest of all Indian reservations, some thirteen million odd acres of beauty, emptiness, and natural resources. But the Navajos are also the biggest of all Indian tribes, with a population of over 125,000.

The traditional Navajo family tends sheep, raises horses or cattle, and lives in a hogan—a roundish, usually hexagonal, dwelling of wood, often covered with earth. In the words of Clyde Kluckhohn:

"The hogan is an excellent simple adaptation to the climate. Its thick walls keep out the cold in winter and, to some extent, heat in summer; the centrally placed fire keeps all parts of the dwelling warm, and there is room for more occupants to sleep around the fire. We [the writers] have found hogans generally more comfortable than the thin-walled cabins of white homesteaders. To the white visitor, it is astonishing how many individuals can eat, sleep, and store many of their possessions within one room not more than twenty-five feet in diameter." (Kluckhohn, p. 45)

Many sheepherding families have several hogans. When one area is grazed out, they simply drive their herd to a new pasture where another hogan stands ready to receive the family. The old primitive "forked stick" hogan is a thing of the past. Besides the traditional hogan with just an iron stove for heating and a kerosene lamp for light, there are now modern hogans in the various settlements, that are large in size, and have electric lights, tapwater, electric kitchen ranges and, in rare cases, even indoor toilets. Navajos expressed their love and respect for their ancestral dwelling by building their Tribal Council, at Window Rock, in the shape of a hogan. Even the gleaming, multi-storied, glass structure of the Navajo Community College at Tsaile is erected in the traditional hexagonal shape.

Unlike the Pueblos, among whom the men do the weaving, it is the Navajo woman who makes the rug, putting up her loom either inside or outside the hogan. As Wharton James observed:

"The greatest charm, however, of these primitive fabrics, is the unrestrained freedom shown by the weaver in her treatment of primitive conventions. To the checkered emblem of the rainbow she adds sweeping rays of color, typifying sunbeams; below the many-angled cloud group, she inserts random pencil lines of rains; or she softens the rigid meander, signifying lightning, with graceful interlacing and shaded tints. Not confining herself alone to these traditional devices...she introduces curious, realistic figures of common objects—her grass brush, wooden weaving fork, a stalk of corn, a bow and arrow...."

Nowadays this also includes trains, automobiles, airplanes, or the Stars and Stripes. Wharton was wrong in one respect—Navajo rugs are often highly sophisticated, not at all "primitive." The weaving of rugs, incidentally, is due to encouragement by early white traders who found it easier to sell rugs than blankets to tourists.

While women weave, it is mostly the men who do the silver-smithing. This art was introduced by the Spaniards in the middle of the nineteenth century, and there is hardly a Navajo man or woman who does not wear a silver and turquoise concho belt, necklace, bracelet, or ring. Good rugs and jewelry are both worth a good deal of money, resulting, unfortunately, in a flood of foreign imitations: cheap Mexican Yei rugs made to look like the real thing, and fake "genuine Indian jewelry" from Hong Kong or Taiwan. In some cases, the silver is not silver and the turquoise is made of plastic.

Most Navajo women still wear the traditional dress—a red, green, or blue velveteen blouse with plenty of silver buttons; a flowery patterned, often pleated skirt; and Navajo-style moccasins. They do their hair in the back with a knot tied with white or red wool. Compared to the Sioux, there are surprisingly few mixed-bloods, and few Navajo-white marriages.

As with other Native American tribes, religion is all-important to the Navajo. In their belief system, there are the Earth-surface people, ordinary men and women, living and dead. And then there are the Holy People, who are holy not in the sense of the Christian missionary, but in the Indian sense of having supernatural powers. At the head of the Holy People stands Changing Woman, the benevolent All-Mother who taught the People all they needed to know. Made pregnant by a sunbeam and by water from a waterfall, Changing Woman gave birth to the Hero Twins—Monster Slayer and Water Child—who are prayed to in most Navajo rituals. It was Changing Woman who gave the Dineh the "Blessing Way," their chief ceremony. Forever young and more comely than even the most beautiful of Earth-surface women, Changing Woman dwells in a magic hogan on the Waters of the West.

Sand paintings are parts of a "sing," which is the Navajo term for a great many curing rituals. To have a "sing," it is necessary to procure the help of a medicine man—a *hatali* or chanter. He is one who brings evil under control, the diviner who diagnoses the cause of illness. His knowledge took many years to acquire. He searches for the cause of evil by "listening," or by looking at stars, or by eating an herb of enlightenment. Sometimes he is a hand-trembler. A hand-trembler's whole body shakes. His trembling hands wander, hesitate, hover over a patch of cornmeal until finally his finger traces upon it some ancient design indicating the cause of the disease and the appropriate chant for the cure.

The sand painting is part of the chant. There are about 500 different sand painting designs for almost as many chants. The patient sits on the painting. The *hatali* transfers some of the sand to the sick one's skin, bringing him in tune with its symbols and power. Thus the human being and the painting are physically united. After the sing, the sand painting is destroyed. During the ritual, the patient's confidence is restored as he or she listens to the words of the chant:

> Happily I recover
> Happily my interior becomes cool
> Happily my eyes regain their power
> Happily my head becomes cool
> Happily my legs regain their power
> Happily I hear again
> Happily for me the spell is taken off!
> Happily may I walk in beauty!

Many Navajo chants are poetry of the highest order, equal to that produced by any other culture in the world. They are haunting, and of almost unearthly beauty. One nineteenth-century writer found "that these ceremonies might vie in allegory, symbolism, and intricacy of ritual with the ceremonies of any people, ancient or modern...that these heathens, pronounced godless and legendless, possessed lengthy myths and traditions—so numerous that one can never hope to collect them all, a pantheon as well stocked with gods and heroes as that of the ancient Greeks and prayers which, for length and repetition, might put a Hebrew prophet to blush....Wonderful songs were found, full of poetic imagery handed down from generation to generation." (Wharton James, pp.125-126)

The Navajo aim, then, is simple. They want to do the right thing, to go through life in the right Dineh way, to live in harmony with their surroundings, to do as Changing Woman had taught. The right way to live is full of taboos of every kind. The Navajo will avoid a tree struck by lightning, never kill a snake, or eat raw meat. Inside the hogan, a Navajo will never step over a sleeping person, nor will a Navajo man have any contact with his mother-in-law if he can help it.

Typically Indian, Navajos are good and loving parents. Before a baby's birth, the father makes a cradleboard in which the newborn will spend the first months of its life. As the baby is placed in it, a special song is chanted:

> I have made a cradleboard for you my
>   son (daughter)
> May you grow to a great old age
> Of the sun's rays I made the back
> Of black clouds I have made the blanket
> Of rainbow I have made the bow
> Of sunbeams have I made the side loops
> Of lightning have I made the lacings
> Of sundogs have I made the footboard
> Of dawn have I made the covering
> Of black dog have I made the bed.

For a girl, upon reaching puberty, an elaborate ritual is performed, one of whose features is a ceremonial foot race.

To the casual observer, the modern Navajos seem to have reason to feel satisfied. Many of them live in modern homes, with a standard of living comparable to their Anglo and Hispanic neighbors. Nontraditional Dineh may be businessmen, telephone repair workers, gas station owners or attendants, farmers, policemen or women, writers for the tribal newspaper, roadworkers, electricians, teachers, tribal officials, doctors, or lawyers. They might run the gigantic wood-processing equipment at the tribal sawmill. They could be college professors. Some earn very good salaries. But the picture is somewhat deceiving. Though many Navajos have made it in the White Man's world, most are still poor. Even those who have been "successfully acculturated," as the official language calls it, are vaguely unfulfilled. A reader of the *Navajo Times* expressed the uneasy feeling of the Native American conforming to an alien life style:

"I have a job, good wages, a house, a car, food on the table and plenty of clothes. Yet, there is something missing in my life. These things should be all I and my family need, but somehow it is not enough.

"I live in a new housing development built on a mesa, where there was only sand, rock and sagebrush a few years back; but I don't know my neighbors. I hardly leave my house to look at the night sky or the sunlight or the sandstone cliffs.

"At night I watch television. My life and the lives of my children are as empty as the programs on television. We live from purchase to purchase—a new car, a new refrigerator; material things which give us the momentary pleasure of new possessions and then leave us wondering what next new thing to look forward to.

"The children ride by bus for hours to go to a brand new school which sticks up from the top of a mesa; an enormous, multicolored box which does not fit the beauty of the high desert landscape.

"My children have hardly learned to read and write at the school. They do not read books. They watch television. What will they do to earn a living when they are grown? Will machines do their reading, writing and arithmetic? If so, what functions will be left to occupy their minds and bodies?

"We become separated from our culture. Our parents, and those in their community are rooted in the land and everything they do and think is related to the land on which they live. We no longer feel this close connection, and so it is hard for us to understand them, just as it is hard for them to understand how it is with us. When we return home, we no longer feel comfortable in the hogan. We are used to running water and supermarket foods, more separation from the weather, more personal privacy and all the other things one becomes accustomed to in a technological society. When it comes time to leave, we are glad to return to the comfort of our civilized home, to the emotional oblivion of television."

This problem is common to all Indians. A Cheyenne, Sioux, Kwakiutl, or Iroquois could have written this letter.

The Navajos are also said to be fortunate because there is coal, oil, and uranium on their reservation. This has not made the individual Navajo rich. The money and royalties are used by the tribe for all the people. With 125,000 to 150,000 of them, the improvements are spread very thinly. Also, natural resources, as used by white technocrats, have proved a curse rather than a blessing. Strip-mining, such as on Black Mesa, has been an ecological disaster and has threatened the people's water supply in a country of little rain. Navajos who worked in the uranium mines are dying prematurely of cancer. It has been said that the Navajos are citizens of an underdeveloped Third World country existing within the United States, with all the attendant problems. The greatest problem at this time is the conflict over Big Mountain. Originally white-manufactured, it is condemned by both Hopi and Dineh traditionalists, and has resulted in the forcible eviction of hundreds of traditional families who are now obliged to live in slums of "ticky-tacky" housing. They are undergoing the trauma so aptly described by the writer to the *Navajo Times*. But, as one anthropologist said: "The Navajo is poor and insecure, but then he is also patently not poor and insecure."

The Navajos are living symbols of human endurance and the will and skill to survive. At the dawn of history they managed to adapt themselves to the harsh conditions of the arctic wasteland. With spears made of wood, their points hardened in fire, they successfully hunted the big-tusked mammoth. They survived the burning deserts, Spanish muskets, and Kit Carson's cannon. They survived the holocaust of Bosque Redondo, the disastrous years of forced livestock reduction, the meddling of missionaries and politicians, and the onrush of white civilization and technology. They are even successfully surviving a particularly big threat: the Anglo tourists. Reduced to 7300 men, women, and children when, after the Long Walk, they returned to their ancestral home, they managed, under the most adverse condition, to increase twenty-fold. I sometimes wonder uneasily what will become of us white superpowered Americans. Will we still be here one hundred, two hundred years hence? I am sure the Navajos will.▷

Navajo lady on horse and long shot of her herd and boys. Canyon de Chelly.

We make only some $1,500 a year. Sheep are our only wealth. So when that government comes in killing our sheep for what they call "over-grazing," then they might just as well kill us along with the sheep.

Navajo lady on horseback, Canyon de Chelly, 1964

Navajo mother with cradleboard.

The whites called our cradleboards "papoose carriers." Very primitive, they said. But now you see white mothers all over using a kind of "primitive papoose carrier." The whites are learning.

Ginger Hillis, 1979

Navajo weaver in Canyon de Chelly.

On our rugs we always leave an opening for the spirits to get out. Navajo rugs are an invention of the white traders. In the old days we wove only blankets, like the striped chief's blankets. Then the traders encouraged us to make rugs. They sold better than blankets. The trader kept most of the money, so my mother told me.

Navajo Weaver at Hubbel's Trading Post

Sand painting in progress.

A sand painting is for curing. It goes with a certain song. It has to be exactly made. During the "sing" the one who is sick sits on the sand painting. After the ceremony the painting is destroyed.

Mitchell, Navajo teacher
Navajo Community College

Old Navajo lady with goat, with cat, and cooking.

I live all alone here with my cat, my lambs, and this little goat. I have to milk-feed the kid because the mother died. The hogan is big enough for just me and the cat. I do everything for myself. But I worry about winter.

Old lady living alone, Lukachukai, Arizona 1979

Near Kayenta, Arizona.

ABOUT THE AUTHOR

Richard Erdoes is the co-author of *Lame Deer: Seeker of Visions*, *American Indian Myths and Legends,* and the author of more than twenty other titles. His most recent work is *A.D. 1000: Living on the Brink of Apocalypse.* He is an Austrian-born historian, ethnographer, and artist, and has contributed illustrations to many magazines, including *Time, Life, Fortune, The New York Times, Smithsonian,* and *Saturday Evening Post.* His photographs have been printed in books published by Time-Life, National Geographic, and Reader's Digest corporations. He was a finalist for the 1981 best Western non-fiction award by Western Writers of America for *Saloons of the Old West.* Erdoes has pursued the protection of indigenous people in North America throughout his life.

BIBLIOGRAPHY

Publications cited throughout the text are listed in the Bibliograpy.

ANDERSON, EDWARD. *Peyote, the Divine Cactus*. Tucson: University of Arizona Press, 1980.

COLLIER, JOHN. *On the Gleaming Way*. Denver: Sage Books, 1949, 1962.

DENSMORE, FRANCES. *Teton Sioux Music*. Smithsonian Institute, Bureau of American Ethnology, Bulletin 61. Washington, DC: Government Printing Office, 1918.

FREUCHEN, PETER. *The Book of the Eskimos*. New York: World Publishing Company, 1961.

JAMES, GEORGE WHARTON. *Indians of the Painted Desert Region*. Boston: Little Brown & Co., 1903.

KLUCKHOHN, CLYDE, and DOROTHEA LEIGHTON. *The Navajo*. Cambridge, MA: Harvard University Press, 1960.

LA BARRE, WESTON. *The Peyote Cult*. Hamden, CT: Shoe String Press, Inc., 1959.

LUMMIS, CHARLES F. *Mesa, Canyon, and Pueblo*. New York: The Century Co., 1925.

SANDOZ, MARI. *These Were the Sioux*. New York: Hastings House, 1961.

STEVENSON, MATILDA COXE. *The Zuni Indians*. Twenty-third Annual Report of the Bureau of American Ethnology. Washington, DC: Smithsonian Institute, 1901-1902.